THE ESSENTIAL
DRACULA

THE ESSENTIAL
DRACULA

by Clare Haworth-Maden

Crescent Books
New York

This 1992 edition published by Crescent Books, distributed by Outlet Book Company, Inc., a Random House Company, 40 Engelhard Avenue Avenel, New Jersey 07001

Produced by Brompton Books Corporation 15 Sherwood Place, Greenwich, CT 06830

ISBN 0-517-06973-3

8 7 6 5 4 3 2 1

Printed and bound in Hong Kong

Page 1: *Bela Lugosi in Dracula,* 1931.
Page 2: *Another victim succumbs to Christopher Lee in* Scars of Dracula.
Right: *Lon Chaney Jnr. contemplates his next meal in* Son of Dracula.

Contents

Birth of the Legend

'The "nosferatu" do not die . . .'

STOKER, *Dracula*

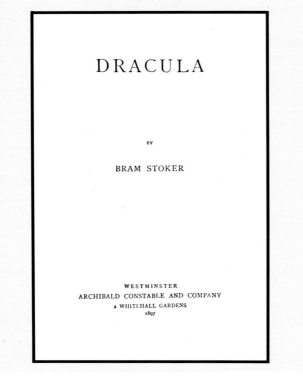

DRACULA

BY

BRAM STOKER

WESTMINSTER
ARCHIBALD CONSTABLE AND COMPANY
2 WHITEHALL GARDENS
1897

Left: *Bela Lugosi – his* Dracula *of 1931 remains the classic interpretation of the role of the King Vampire.*

Above: *Title page of the first edition of Bram Stoker's* Dracula. *Its restrained appearance gives little indication of the horrors to follow.*

Bram Stoker unleashed Count Dracula upon a horrified, yet enthralled, public in 1897. The book has never been out of print since, and his incredible story, retold in countless films, has continued to terrify generations of movie-goers. The King-Vampire from Transylvania has captured popular imagination like few other demons of the occult. There can be few people for whom the name 'Dracula' does not conjure up a sinister, threatening figure, his black evening dress contrasting sharply with his pallid face, and his pronounced white fangs dripping with fresh, crimson blood.

Dracula is, after all, only a fictitious character, yet he has managed to insinuate himself into our unconsciousness, ready to appear at our weakest and most vulnerable moments. Why is his hold on us so great? Is it because we secretly fear that there might be some truth in his story?

The key lies in our fascination with the supernatural: 'the supernatural' being any abnormal event or being whose existence or occurrence cannot be accounted for by the rational mind or by the laws of nature. Belief in, and fear of, the supernatural, have prevailed since the advent of man. The primitive mind put down unusual events to the work of 'good' or 'evil' supernatural beings, the allocation depending on their positive or negative consequences. As the centuries passed, these beliefs were harnessed by the world's great religions, 'God' and 'miracles' being positive supernatural forces, 'Satan' and 'the devil's work' representing the antithesis. Thus, absolute faith in the teaching of the Bible, the Koran, or other religious works, guided believers in accepting the inexplicable. Furthermore, as mankind became increasingly enlightened, many 'supernatural' phenomena were discovered to have perfectly logical explanations within the scientific order.

7

Nowadays, there are few instances of the supernatural which cannot be given a feasible scientific explanation, yet many people persist in retaining a half-belief in the supernatural (although they might be loathe to admit it). Psychoanalysts have advanced several hypotheses: Sigmund Freud stressed the importance of man's unconscious mind, while Carl Jung emphasized the collective nature of the subconscious. So while superstitious tales and beliefs have been passed down through generations, kept alive by means of oral and written communcation, might we not also possess a mental collective 'folk memory', inherited from our less sophisticated, more credulous ancestors?

Dracula, as we know him, sprang from the pen of Bram Stoker, a Dublin-born civil servant. His first book, with the unprepossessing title *The Duties of Clerks at Petty Sessions in Ireland*, cannot be further removed from the Gothic tale of vampirism with which he was to make his name, yet it was this unlikely author who would sensationalize the threat of the 'undead.' Stoker's chilling masterpiece is prefaced with these words:

All needless matters have been eliminated, so that a history almost at variance with the possibilities of latter-day belief may stand forth as simple fact.

By means of a series of journals, written by different hands and interspersed with newspaper articles, letters and telegrams, Stoker weaves an intricate framework of plausibility and rationality within which the story of Dracula unfolds.

The account begins as Jonathan Harker, a recently qualified solicitor, travels to the Transylvanian castle of his client, a nobleman who wishes to purchase an estate in England. He is perplexed to notice that when he makes his destination known to innkeepers and fellow passengers, all cross themselves fervently and try to dissuade him from his purpose. When their efforts fail, they press unusual gifts upon him: a crucifix, garlic, the wild rose and a sprig of mountain ash.

After a hair-raising journey on Walpurgis Night when, according to superstition, 'all the evil things in the world . . . have full sway,' Harker arrives at Dracula's castle, where he is welcomed by the Count, whose hand is 'as cold as ice – more like the hand of a dead than a living man.' On later observation, he notes Dracula's sharp white teeth, which protrude over his ruddy lips, the hairs which grow in the center of his palms, his sharpened nails and rank breath. Furthermore, the Count does not eat and reserves his discussions with Harker to the hours after midnight, disappearing with alacrity at cockcrow. There are no mirrors in Castle Dracula, and when Harker uses his own to shave, he is startled to find that on Dracula's approach he can see no reflection; he cuts himself and Dracula, transformed by the sight of blood, makes a grab for his throat, but is repulsed by Harker's crucifix.

Each night the Count visits Harker, and speaks of his brave and mighty ancestors, as well as his future home in England. He warns Harker, for his own safety, not to explore the castle. However, his suspicions aroused, having seen Dracula crawl down the castle wall, his cape spread out like wings, Harker disobeys and encounters three beautiful women – vampires – to whom he nearly surrenders himself. 'Saved' by Dracula, who appeases them with a kidnapped child, Harker becomes a prisoner in the castle and realizes that he is doomed to die. He manages to break free and finds a chapel housing 50 great boxes, one of which contains the Count, showing no signs of life. On this instance he is frightened away, but later returns to make a terrible discovery:

it seemed as if the whole awful creature were simply gorged with blood . . . This was the being I was helping to transfer to London, where, perhaps for centuries to come, he might, amongst its teeming millions, satiate his lust for blood, and create a new and ever widening circle of semi-demons to batten on the helpless.

He tries to kill Dracula with a spade but, alas, fails. As his account ends, he is resolved to escape, rather than be sacrificed to the three female vampires.

Meanwhile, oblivious to his ordeal in Transylvania, Harker's fiancée, Mina, arrives in Whitby in Yorkshire to visit her friend, Lucy Westenra. Lucy has received three proposals of marriage: from John Seward, an earnest young doctor in charge of a lunatic asylum at Carfax in Purfleet; from Quincy P. Morris, a dashing Texan – both of whom she regretfully refuses – and from Arthur Holmwood, whom she accepts.

Lucy and Mina settle down to enjoy carefree days, but the atmosphere darkens when Lucy begins to sleepwalk. One night, a violent storm pitches a Russian schooner, the *Demeter* on to the shore. A huge dog leaps ashore and makes off into the night: Dracula has arrived in England, did they but know it. On inspection of the ship, a dead seaman is found lashed

Above: 'In the moonlight opposite me were three young women . . .': Dracula's vampiric harem in Universal's 1931 movie.

Right: Piccadilly Circus, London, in 1894. Dracula apparently found Piccadilly a desirable address, buying a house here in which to lodge some of his coffins.

Left: Bram Stoker, the civil servant whose vivid Irish imagination created a terrifying tale of vampirism.

to the ship's wheel and, in the hold, 50 great boxes of earth, which are legally assigned to a local solicitor. The dead captain's log tells of the disappearance, one by one, of his crew, and the presence on board of an evil being.

Shortly afterwards, Lucy walks to the churchyard in her sleep where Mina discovers her, lying above the grave of a suicide, with a strange man bending over her. On escorting her home, Mina notices two puncture marks on her neck and is disturbed by a persistent bat knocking at the window. The following day Mina has word of Jonathan, who is recovering from his ordeal in a Budapest hospital, and leaves Lucy to be by his side. They marry, and he hands her his diary, only to be read in case of emergency.

In England, Dr Seward is becoming intrigued by the case of one of his patients, Renfield, a 'zoophagous [life-eating] maniac,' whose habit it is to encourage spiders to eat flies, sparrows to eat the spiders, and finally, having been denied a cat, eating the sparrows himself. Suddenly he loses interest in his obsession, explaining that 'the Master is at hand.' He escapes to the chapel of the mansion adjoining the asylum, where 50 boxes of earth have recently been delivered, for Carfax is Dracula's newly purchased English estate.

Lucy's condition deteriorates: she is bloodless, lethargic and is plagued by nightmares. Concerned, Seward summons his friend, Professor Van Helsing, an expert on obscure diseases, who pronounces Lucy's case to be 'a matter of life and death.' Lucy receives blood transfusions from Holmwood, Seward, Morris and Van Helsing in turn, for she is literally being drained of blood. Not even garlic flowers can protect her now, and somehow her teeth appear longer and sharper . . . Finally she dies, yet, inexplicably, in death she looks far healthier than she did in life.

Far left: *Castle Bran, Romania, popularly believed to be Vlad the Impaler's castle.*

Left: *Highgate Cemetery, London, haunted by the undead Lucy.*

Below left: *The ruins of the Abbey at Whitby, North Yorkshire, scene of Lucy's nocturnal assignations with Count Dracula.*

Below: *The Vampyre by Philip Burne-Jones. The Victorians were well aware of the vampire's various guises – and of its threat.*

Mina and Jonathan return to England to start their married life. However, while in London, Jonathan is shattered by a glimpse of Dracula, apparently grown young, in the heart of Piccadilly. Disturbed, Mina reads his diary. Unsure whether to believe his incredible experiences, she consults Van Helsing, who assures her that they are true. The latter has more urgent matters to attend to: a 'bloofer lady' is abducting small children on Hampstead Heath (close to Lucy's grave) and although later discovered alive, the children are found to have puncture marks on their throats. Van Helsing fears the worst, and he and Seward visit Lucy's tomb, only to find it empty. As the cock crows, they see her shadowy figure return, clutching a child. Later, she is found restored to her coffin, blooming with health. Van Helsing convinces Seward, Morris and Holmwood (now Lord Godalming, following the death of his father) that Lucy is 'undead.' They nobly set her soul to rest by driving a stake through her heart, cutting off her head and filling her mouth with garlic, after which they vow to save the world from Dracula.

These four, together with the Harkers, collate their journals and the Count's dastardly plan becomes clear. They discover that 29 of the 50 boxes have vanished from the Carfax chapel and determine to find them and sterilize them with the Host, so that Dracula cannot find refuge within them. The missing boxes are traced to Mile End in the East End of London, Bermondsey in south London, and Piccadilly in the west. These, along with the batch in Purfleet, mean that Dracula has havens on all four points of the compass.

Renfield, having become increasingly disturbed, is found half crushed to death. Before he dies, he reveals that Dracula had 'bought' him with the promise of as much life to consume as he desired. Renfield, however, is outraged by the realization that the Count has vampirized Mina, and struggles with him, thus receiving his fatal injuries. Mina is discovered being forced to drink the Count's blood: she is now under his command; a brand, seared into her forehead by the holy touch of the Host (an attempt by Van Helsing to protect her) is a constant reminder of her enslavement.

A council of war is held and Van Helsing, in his idiosyncratic English, warns the others of the terrible might of their enemy:

The 'nosferatu' do not die like the bee when he sting once. He is only stronger; and being stronger, have yet more power to work evil. This vampire which is amongst us is of himself so strong in person as twenty men; he is of cunning more than mortal, for his cunning be the growth of ages; he have still the aids of necromancy, which is, as his etymology imply, the divination by the dead, and all the dead that he can come nigh to are for him at command; he is brute and more than brute; he is devil in callous, and the heart of him is not; he can, within limitations, appear at will, when and where, and in any of the forms that are to him; he can, within his range, direct the elements: the storm, the fog, the thunder; he can command all the meaner things: the rat, and the owl, and the bat – moth, and the fox, and the wolf; he can grow and become small and he can at times vanish and come unknown.

The odds seem insuperable, but Van Helsing assures the group that despite his superhuman powers, Dracula can be overcome, for in some respects his mind is that of a child.

Accordingly, each of the Count's addresses are visited and his earthboxes sterilized, but one box is missing, and one box is enough . . . Dracula has escaped his hunters. In desperation, Mina volunteers to be hypnotized and reveals, through telepathy, that Dracula is on a ship, bound for Transylvania. Through exhaustive detective work, Dracula is pinpointed to the *Czarina Catherine*, bound for Eastern Europe.

The vampire hunt begins: via Paris, to Varna and Galatz. The hunters divide into pairs, Mina and Van Helsing traveling together. The closer they get to Dracula's castle, the more secretive and withdrawn Mina becomes. Once in sight of the castle, the three vampire women appear, and try to entice her to join them, but she is prevented from doing so by a sacred circle drawn around her by Van Helsing, through which she cannot pass. Even Van Helsing nearly succumbs to the deadly fascination of these vampiresses, but resists and bravely carries out the grisly task of laying their souls to rest. Following a fierce battle with the gypsies who are carrying Dracula's coffin home, during which Morris is fatally wounded, Dracula is destroyed and his body crumbles into dust, but not before it has registered an ineffable look of peace. With his demise, Mina is released from the vampire's thrall, and the stigmatizing brand disappears from her forehead.

This, then, is Stoker's tale of Dracula, complete with happy ending – or is it? Who knows how many of Dracula's cohorts might even now be stalking the earth, undead? Much of the fascination of *Dracula*, underlined by the presentation of the story as a collation of pieces of 'factual' evidence, comes from our niggling uncertainty as to whether it might, indeed, be based on fact. After all, Quincy P. Morris refers to the blood-sucking vampire bats (*Desmondontidae*) which we know inhabit Central America; might not other aspects of the story also be true?

A hideous, animated corpse, who leaves his tomb in order to drink the blood of its human victims, the vampire has been part of popular folklore for centuries. Most cultures have their versions of the vampire, although their characteristics may vary from land to land. A truly international superstition, early forms of vampirism were chronicled in ancient Greece and countries as diverse as India, China and Russia. However, it is in Central and Eastern Europe, where, 'every known superstition in the world is gathered into the horseshoe of the Carpathians' and particularly in what is now Romania, that the vampire myth is most deeply rooted.

Stoker's vampire is not entirely true to the vampire of popular legend, although vampiric attributes varied considerably from culture to culture. Stoker clothed Dracula in funereal black; most vampires wear the shrouds in which they were buried. Stoker does not enlighten us about how, or why, Dracula became a vampire; international myths list a variety of reasons for becoming 'undead': death in a state of sin; wickedness during life; suicide; a cat jumping over the coffin before burial; the misfortune of being born on Christmas Day; being born with teeth; any manifestly 'different' appearance: having red hair or blue eyes, for example, in countries where such attributes are not the norm. The parallels with the witch hunt are striking: anyone who did not conform, physically or behaviorally, was in danger of being branded 'a vampire' or 'a witch' and was accordingly persecuted – often to death.

According to Stoker, Count Dracula possesses the following common vampiric attributes: extreme pallor and emaciation, except when he has feasted upon blood, whereafter he appears bloated, with ruddy lips and a blooming complexion; talon-like fingernails; hairy palms; sharp canine teeth which protrude over the lips; strong hypnotic powers; abnormal strength, control over the elements; power over 'mean' animals, such as the rat; the ability to change his size and pass through solid matter; the ability to metamorphose into another form, such as a bat or wolf; foul breath; nocturnal vision; the lack of a shadow or reflection and, of course, his need to slake his diabolical thirst with human blood.

Despite his supernatural abilities, however, the vampire has certain limitations which mean that he can be confronted and vanquished by humankind. He may not enter a dwelling unless invited and his power ceases at dawn. He can only change form at noon, sunrise or sunset and he cannot cross running water. As Lucy's misfortune shows, virtue and innocence offer no protection, but garlic, the wild rose and mountain ash, a consecrated silver bullet, a crucifix or any other sacred object, may render the vampire powerless. To destroy him, a wooden stake should be driven through his heart (this was probably derived from the common practice of staking dead criminals in order to keep their spirits pinned down), his head should be cut off and his mouth filled with garlic. Finally, the grisly remains and the coffin should be burned.

Stoker drew many of these characteristics from the 'nosferatu' or 'strigoi' of traditional Slavic myth, adding a few embellishments of his own and throwing in a soupçon of werewolf for good measure. Myth certainly backs up Stoker's Dracula, but what of history? As we shall see, he had another reason for giving Dracula a home where, as he put it 'the bloodsucking vampire hovered the longest.'

By 1878 Stoker had tired of the civil service and was persuaded by his friend Henry Irving, the greatest actor of his day, to manage both his Lyceum Theatre in London and Irving himself. Stoker accompanied him on theatrical tours, and holidayed with him in Whitby in Yorkshire, where he based much of the action in *Dracula*. Another holiday venue, Cruden Bay, near Aberdeen, was to provide the inspiration for Dracula's castle, whose description is remarkably similar to that at Cruden Bay. It is known that Stoker (like Van Helsing) did much research at the British Museum in London, but the main source for his vampiric creation comes from a book published in 1820 which he frequently borrowed from Whitby's public library. The *Account of the principalities of Wallachia and Moldavia with political observations relative to them* by William Wilkinson, contains a history of the life of Dracula, Prince Vlad V of Wallachia (1431-76).

Left: *Not for the first time,
Christopher Lee meets his end,
impaled on a stake in* Dracula
AD 1972.

Left: Frank Langella made a dashing and romantic Count in Dracula, 1979. This movie was keen to emphasize the King Vampire's appeal to his unfortunate female victims.

Left: Vlad *the Impaler enjoying his lunch in a 1499 woodcut, printed by Ambrosius Huber of Nuremburg.*

Right: *Thomas Phillips' 1813 portrait of the romantic Lord Byron in Greek dress, upon whom John Polidori is believed to have based* The Vampyre.

Below left: *A fifteenth-century woodcut portraying Vlad the Impaler, who, according to one biographer, 'was in life a most wonderful man . . .'*

Whatever else he may have been, Vlad 'Tepes' ('the Impaler') was not a vampire. Born into a noble family, Vlad inherited membership of the Order of the Dragon (from which the name Dracula derives [*draco* is Latin for dragon], as does Dracula's wearing of the dragon cape), sworn to fight the Turkish infidel. In the course of these crusades, Dracula was to display his genius for military strategy. He was, however, also a cruel sadist responsible, it is said, for the deaths of more than 100,000 people. His favorite practice was to subject his victims to a slow and agonising death by impalement on sharpened spikes. Stoker paid Dracula a suitably backhanded compliment: 'he was in life a most wonderful man. Soldier, statesman and alchemist . . . He had a mighty brain, a learning beyond compare, and a heart that knew no fear and no remorse.' Dracula met a deservedly violent end, but the sheer magnitude of the horror of his tyrannical rule meant that his deeds were never forgotten. After his death a spate of pamphlets chronicled his cruelty in nauseating detail. *About the wild bloodthirsty berserker Dracula*, printed in 1499 by Ambrosius Huber of Nuremburg, did not find it difficult to speak ill of the dead:

> all those whom he had taken captive, men and women, young and old, children, he had impaled on the hill by the chapel . . . and under them he proceeded to eat at table and get his pleasure that way.

By combining a verifiable historical figure with the more nebulous form of the vampire, Stoker infused a certain authenticity into his fictional Count. However, credibility alone, even combined with the mysteries of the occult, would not have been enough to ensure the book's everlasting appeal: it was the incorporation of 'Gothic' atmosphere which transformed *Dracula* into a classic. In terms of success, *Dracula* is on a par with Mary Shelley's *Frankenstein* and, unlike most tales of the Gothic genre, the popularity of these two books has survived and flourished up to the present day.

The first English vampire novel was a product of the famous occasion when Lord Byron challenged his doctor, John Polidori, Percy Shelley and Shelley's wife, Mary to write a terrifying ghost story. The events of that single evening (when, appropriately, a heart-stopping thunderstorm raged outside) were to produce two of the genre's best-known exponents, *Frankenstein* (1818) and John Polidori's *The Vampyre*, published in 1819. The latter's subtitle ('A tale by Lord Byron') misled the public into believing that Byron was the author. While Byron had, indeed, provided Polidori with the germ of the story, 'Lord Ruthven' (the 'vampyre') was an uncomfortably accurate physical portrayal of Byron himself, and Byron speedily disassociated himself from both the authorship and the author.

The Vampyre initiated a vampire craze, kept alive by Thomas Peckett Priest's penny-dreadful, *Varney the Vampire* (1847). European writers, too, reaped the success of the public's avid flirtation with vampirism. Following the success of Charles Nodier's melodrama *Le Vampire* (1820), for example, there was hardly a theater in Paris not running a vampire play. Even Goethe explored vampirism, in his ballad *The Bride of Corinth* (1798). The genre was given an additional twist by Joseph Sheridan Le Fanu, whose *Carmilla* of 1871 added a new element: that of the female vampire. The story tells of the beautiful Carmilla who, rescued by the innocent young Laura from a wagon wreck, comes to exert an unhealthy fascination over her. 'Car-

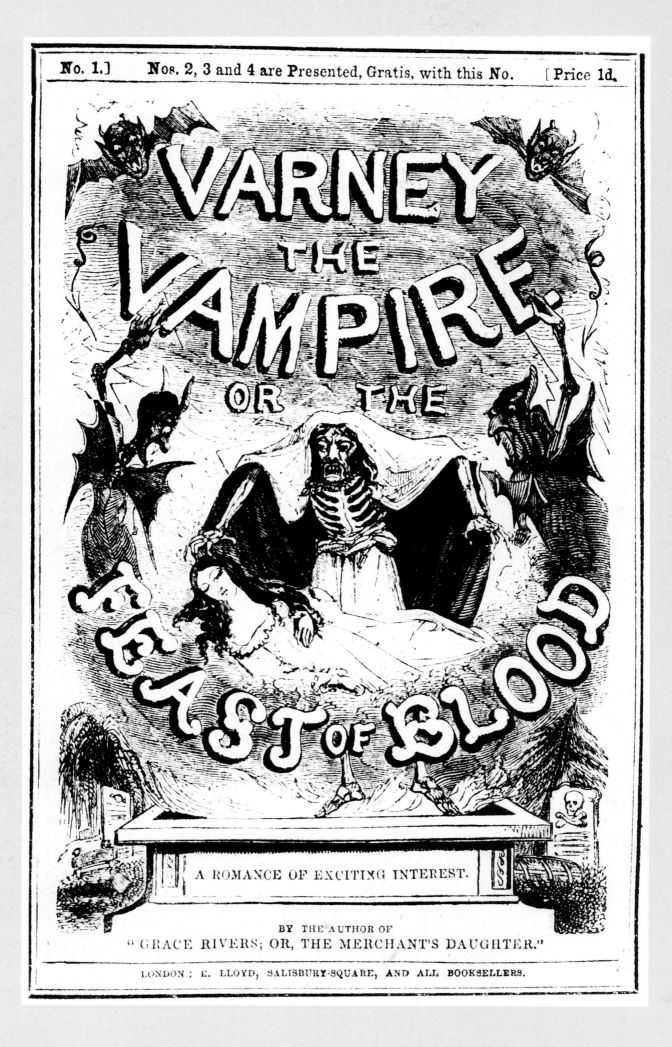

milla' is revealed to be none other than the Countess Mircalla Karnstein, who has been walking the earth for centuries as a vampire, preying upon young girls. She is eventually destroyed in the traditional manner, by means of the stake, decapitation and cremation.

That Stoker had read *Carmilla* is indisputable: after his death his widow, Florence, published a short story, originally intended for inclusion in *Dracula*, elements of which show remarkable similarity to *Carmilla*. The chapter elaborates upon Harker's journey to Castle Dracula on Walpurgis Night. Attracted by the romantic landscape, Harker dismisses his reluctant coachman and finds himself in a graveyard, where he discovers a tomb whose inscription reads: 'Countess Dolingen of Gratz in Styria sought and found death 1801 – The Dead Travel Fast.' Forced by appalling weather to find shelter in the tomb, he sees a beautiful woman, apparently asleep on a bier. Harker loses consciousness and awakes to feel a wolf lying on his breast, licking his throat ominously. He is saved from being savaged by the arrival of a brigade of soldiers, alerted by a note received by his innkeeper 'Be careful of my guest – his safety is most precious to me . . . , Dracula.'

Stoker may have jested that his ghastly Count was conceived during a nightmare, brought on by overindulgence in seafood, but as we have seen, he was indebted to a multitude of sources. *Dracula* comprises a potent mixture of fact, fantasy and atmospheric horror, which enabled it to surpass any of its literary vampiric predecessors. As a contemporary book review commented, 'In seeking a parallel to this weird, powerful and horrid story, our minds revert to such tales as *The Mysteries of Udolpho*, *Frankenstein*, *Wuthering Heights*, *The Fall of the House of Usher* and *Marjery of Quelher*. But *Dracula* is even more appalling in its gloomy fascination than any of these.'

Left: *The title page of Thomas Peckett Priest's popular* Varney the Vampyre *or* The Feast of Blood. *'A romance of exciting interest.'*

Above: *John Polidori, author of* The Vampyre, *published in 1819, the first tale of vampirism printed in English.*

Right: *Sir Francis Varney, villain of* Varney the Vampyre, *threatens a swooning female victim.*

Classic Draculas

'Vampirism is a subject which is suited to the cinema like hardly no other;

after all, now and again there are people up there on the screen who have

been dead for decades, the undead, and the audience sits in the dark just as

the vampire himself sets to work in the dark'

ULRICH KUROWSKI, *Lexicon Film*, 1973

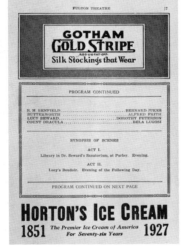

Left: *A classic pose from a 1948 theater production of* Dracula.

Above: *The original program of the Fulton Theater, New York, announcing the presentation of* Dracula: the Vampire Play *in 1927, featuring Bela Lugosi and Edward van Sloan, both of whom would later make the move to cinema.*

Although the literary version of *Dracula* sent a frisson of morbid excitement through its nineteenth century readers, it was Dracula's debut on the silver screen which ensured the Count's immortalization.

The bridge from novel to film was the theater. The first stage version of *Dracula* took place only a few days after the book's publication; the playwright, Stoker himself. *Dracula, or the Un-dead* was an unmitigated disaster; not even Stoker's great friend Henry Irving could bring himself to commend it. The problems of translating the book's spooky atmosphere to the stage discouraged most writers from even attempting another dramatization until Hamilton Deane (head of the Hamilton Deane Company and one-time member of Henry Irving's troupe) turned his attention to the task.

Dean's play *Dracula*, was first performed at the Grand Theatre, Derby in 1924. By judiciously cutting many of the difficult elements contained in the book, Deane avoided the mistakes made in Stoker's dreadful adaptation. The play was an instant success and it was still drawing crowds after its opening at the Little Theatre, London, on Valentine's Day in 1927. The young Raymond Huntley replaced the play's original leading man, Edmund Blake, bringing considerable éclat to the role, with the result that, as the *Evening News* put it, *Dracula* has gone on drinking blood nightly.'

The play had an important influence on our visualization of Dracula. While Stoker's Count possessed a 'black moustache and pointed beard' and dressed in black, Deane did away with these characteristics and instead gave Dracula the now-familiar clean-shaven (green-hued) face, full evening dress, and a swirling black opera cape. It did not pass unnoticed that the revamped Dracula bore a striking resemblance to Deane himself, and it was suspected that, by basing Dracula upon himself, he had intended to play the starring role.

Dracula was a box-office smash and, in 1927, an American producer, Horace Liveright, recognizing its potential for the American market, bought the rights to the play and requested its revision. Deane enlisted the services of the writer John L Balderston and the resulting production opened at the Fulton Theater in New York later that year; in the lead an exotically-named Hungarian émigré, Bela Lugosi.

There was a poignant postscript to the dramatization of Dracula. In 1939 Deane finally cast himself in the role of Dracula, with the result that the play's writer played the leading role in the Lyceum Theatre in London, the theater which Stoker, creator of Dracula, had managed. Furthermore, during the course of the performance, the audience was thrilled to watch Bela Lugosi, whose screen portrayal of Dracula had by then made him a household name, salute Deane on stage.

However, despite its popularity, the theatrical version of Dracula, while a masterly adaptation, was never going to be able to compete with the medium of film, with a vast range of atmospheric photographic effects at its disposal. But in the 1920s, when Dracula was playing to packed theaters in London, movie-making was still in its infancy. The first Dracula film actually preceded Deane's play but, unlike the play, whose title character is instantly recognizable to today's Dracula aficionados, the vampire in Nosferatu: Eine Symphonie des Grauens [Nosferatu: a Symphony of Terror] (Prana, 1922) is strikingly different from Stoker's creation.

Above: Lil Dagover and Conrad Veidt in The Cabinet of Dr Caligari, a landmark of German Expressionist film-making.

Above right: Max Schreck, the hideous 'Count Orlok' of F W Murnau's 1922 masterpiece Nosferatu, a precursor to Dracula.

Right: Nosferatu had Count Orlok vaporising at sunrise, an influential innovation, both in film and in vampire lore.

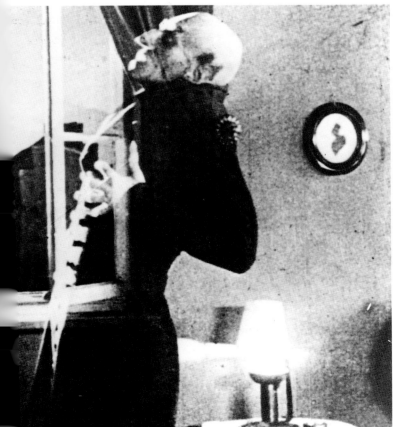

The remarkable silent horror films which came out of Germany in the 1920s reflect the morbid, eschatological *Zeitgeist* of the period following World War I. The defeat of Germany after a long and debilitating war, the humiliating Treaty of Versailles, coupled with the economic hardship and social and political instability of the postwar years, coincided with an artistic explosion, marked in particular by Expressionism, and carried over into film. *The Cabinet of Dr Caligari* (Decla film, 1919), which dealt with hypnotism and murder, signaled the breaking away from the naturalism of the theater into a world of insanity, made possible by film. Liberated from convention, the German producers of the 1920s released a string of macabre, psychologically disturbing Expressionist 'horror' films, including *The Golem*, *Waxworks*, *Warning Shadows*, *The Hands of Orloc* and, of course, *Nosferatu*. These exercises in terror perfectly reflected the prevailing escapist taste for mysticism, dismal fantasy and decadence. Thus, just as Stoker's *Dracula* appealed to the contemporary appetite for black romanticism, so the nihilist *Nosferatu* is a product of its time.

Nosferatu, released in 1922, was directed by FW Murnau, who already had *Der Januskopf* (1920) (a version of the Jekyll and Hyde story) to his credit. Inspired by Stoker's work, but reluctant to pay royalties on *Dracula*, Murnau made extensive changes to Stoker's story, changing the Count's name to 'Orlok' and transferring the setting from Transylvania and England to Germany. However, despite these and other alterations, the film was so clearly based on *Dracula* that Stoker's widow successfully sued for breach of copyright and, in 1925, Prana withdrew the film from circulation. Thankfully, a few copies of *Nosferatu* survived the court's destruction order and it is still occasionally screened today.

Despite the legally proven similarities to *Dracula*, *Nosferatu* is in many ways entirely contrary to its precursor. Max Schreck's portrayal of the Count was based more on the foul, decaying vampire of traditional folklore than Stoker's more urbane version. The aptly named Schreck (literally translated from German, 'Schreck' means 'fright') presented a hideous picture: bald, cadaverous, with claw-like hands and sharpened incisor, rather than canine, teeth. Murnau also introduced other aberrations from the story, some of which would become part of modern vampire lore: Orlok's victims were not to become 'undead' following his bite, but would die; furthermore, the sun's rays are deadly to Murnau's vampire, and Orlok meets his end by vaporizing at sunrise. The Expressionist slant to the film, and some stunning imagery (shot on location rather than on stage sets), coupled with the overwhelming ghastliness of Orlok, all serve to make *Nosferatu* a truly memorable masterpiece.

By the 1930s, European movie-making was in decline. America had established itself at the forefront of cinema, complementing its money and technology with the creativity of the many directors and actors recruited from Europe. The advent of sound and the American domination of the film market ensured that, with one notable exception, the vampire films of the 1930s would be monopolized by Hollywood. The exception was Carl Dreyer's *Vampyre*, released in 1932 in Germany, and based on Le Fanu's collection of stories contained in *In a Glass Darkly*, including *Carmilla*. A hauntingly evocative piece, focusing on a female vampire, *Vampyre's* disturbing beauty is of an artistic standard sadly lacking in many American films of the era. However, artistic excellence is rarely a prerequisite for box-office success, and the most popular horror films of the 1930s were to come from the stable of Universal Pictures.

Universal's association with the horror genre had begun in the 1920s with, among others, *The Hunchback of Notre Dame* (1923) and *The Phantom of the Opera* (1925), both screen adaptations of Gothic novels, a trend which it was to continue with the release in the same year – 1931 – of *Dracula* and *Frankenstein*. The cinematic potential of a sound version of *Dracula* was underlined, in the minds of the studio executives, by the success of Hamilton Deane's play.

It was originally intended that Lon Chaney, 'the man of a thousand faces,' an established American 'horror' star who had portrayed a vampire in *London after Midnight* in 1927, should play Dracula, but his death in 1930 left the role uncast, until Tod Browning, the film's director, proposed the little-known Hungarian actor, Bela Lugosi, for the part. Lugosi was already earmarked for a part in *Frankenstein*, but Browning argued that he would be far better suited to *Dracula*: it was felt that his Hungarian background would help audiences to identify the actor with the fictional Transylvanian Count, with the additional bonus that he had been frightening audiences for years in the very play upon which the film would be based.

The casting of Lugosi as Dracula was inspired. Adopting the characteristics of Deane's Dracula, not only did he look the part with his stark-white face, jet black hair and staring eyes, his cupid-bow mouth and the long, elegant hands which

Left: 'The Master' metes out brutal punishment to the deranged Renfield. Bela Lugosi and Dwight Frye in Dracula, 1931.

Far left: Lon Chaney Sr., 'The man of a thousand faces', assumed the role of a vampire in London after Midnight in 1927. First choice for the Universal Dracula, his death left the title role of the movie uncast.

Right: A promotional poster announcing the release of Dracula in 1931. This film would become the definitive vampire movie.

Left: Bela Lugosi approaches his sleeping victim in Dracula, 1931. A locked door cannot keep the vampire out.

he used to such effect, but, in spite of Boris Karloff's comment that 'Bela's tragedy was that he never learned the language,' his strong foreign accent was a definite advantage. No American actor could have convincingly eked out his celebrated opening words, 'I . . . am . . . Dra-cu-la,' to five seconds. Elliott Stein sums up the appeal of Lugosi's performance in the first sound version of Dracula: 'The film is graced from beginning to end with some of the most distinctive music ever heard – the voice of Bela Lugosi . . . Lugosi's unforgettable accent, offbeat phrasing and minatory pauses – as much as his hypnotic eyes – were essential to his aura of dignified balefulness.' Furthermore, in contrast to Max Schreck's monstrous portrayal, Lugosi's Dracula was disturbingly human: civilized, attractive and well versed in the social graces.

The film also featured Edward Van Sloan (as Van Helsing), Dwight Frye (Renfield), David Manners (Harker) and Helen Chandler (Mina). While the audience's response to the film was that of delighted terror, critical reviews were mixed. There was much praise for Karl Freund's brilliant camera work in the German style, but it was felt that the creepy atmosphere he conjured up was seriously undermined by the verbosity and plodding pace of the script and the fact that much of the crucial action took place off-screen. The *Dracula* of 1931 does not stand up to the sophisticated standards of modern cinema audiences, nor, sadly, does Lugosi's style of acting: its hammy melodrama might have been suited to the theater and have been accepted by the less demanding viewers of the time, but nowadays it comes across as ludicrous. However, the film was massively influential and set the terms of reference for future vampire films, just as Stoker's book had standardized vampirism itself.

Tragically, Lugosi's suave interpretation of Count Dracula was so compelling that, not only would it become accepted as a yardstick for future portrayals, but Lugosi would become a victim of its success. He would be condemned to attempt to reproduce his famous performance time and time again (in films such as *Mark of the Vampire* (1935), *Frankenstein Meets the Wolf Man* (1943) and *Return of the Vampire* (1943), with only infrequent escapes into other, generally bad, roles, until his re-enactments became reduced to the level of parody. The *Dracula* of 1931 was the highlight of his career and public identification of Lugosi with Dracula was so great that, encouraged at first by studio pressure to promote this image for publicity purposes as part of his personal life, he later (voluntarily) gave interviews reclining in a coffin. Beset by financial and marital problems and addicted to morphine, Lugosi died in 1956. His final request was that he should be buried with his opera cape.

Although other actors would assume Dracula's fabled mantle after Lugosi's decline, it seemed that none could capture the mesmerizing fascination that Lugosi, at his best, could exert over the public. Furthermore, while Universal's ingenious use of lighting and basic sets had much to commend it in the 1930s, it became obvious in the years following World War II that this approach was tired and unsuited to the more sophisticated requirements of postwar audiences.

Movie fans still wished to be agreeably scared, and although America could no longer fulfil this desire adequately, England could. Hammer Films had released *The Curse of Frankenstein* in 1957, to massive acclaim. The film heralded a breakthrough from the increasingly stifling limitations of Hollywood's treatment of horror, and satisfied the modern public's demand for terror, realism, action and titillation. Hammer's dramatic 'Gothic' sets, vivid use of color, sexual suggestiveness and liberal sprinklings of artificial blood catered admirably for this taste; after decades of Hammer films based on these criteria, it is difficult to imagine a time when the formula was refreshingly new.

Dracula and Frankenstein always seem to go in tandem and it is therefore unsurprising that on seeking a follow-up to match, or better, the commercial success of *The Curse of Frankenstein*, Hammer's executives should hit upon the idea of remaking *Dracula*.

Left: Bela Lugosi and Dwight Frye in Dracula, 1931. The Dracula of Bram Stoker's novel was generally clad in black 'without a single speck of color about him.' Lugosi's formal evening dress not only emphasized the Count's magnetism, but set the standard for numerous later Draculas.

Below left: Van Helsing (Edward van Sloan) examining Mina (Helen Chandler) for signs of the vampire's bite, Dracula, 1931.

Right: Carlos Villarias and Eduardo Aruzamena in the Spanish language version of Dracula, shot on the same sets and released in the same year as Universal's 1931 classic.

Below right: Foiled again – Edward van Sloan causes Bela Lugosi a moment of displeasure, Dracula, 1931.

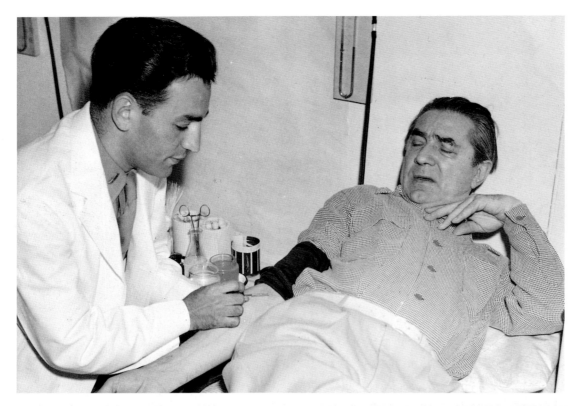

Left: Universal encouraged Bela Lugosi to promote his 'Dracula' persona. Here, in a role reversal, Lugosi donates blood in Los Angeles.

Below left: Bela Lugosi and Carol Borland in Mark of the Vampire, 1935.

Right: Christopher Lee bare his teeth in Hammer's Horror of Dracula (also known simply as Dracula), 1958. It is one of the best Dracula movies to date.

By happy chance, Christopher Lee, the tall, gaunt actor who had brought Frankenstein's monster to life in 1957, once divested of the hideous make-up, looked like promising vampire material. Rather than try to imitate Lugosi, Hammer's make-up artist reverted to Stoker's description of the Count. Lee was given a magnificent head of gray-streaked hair, combed back from a widow's peak, and was dressed entirely in black. A modest pair of fangs and red contact lenses (which caused Lee acute discomfort), were the only concessions to the supernatural and the total, restrained look would have found favor with Stoker himself. Lee was required to play out the athletic agility and enormous strength of the original Dracula which fortuitously also pleased a public eager for action.

Left: John van Eyssen prepares to
'release' Valerie Grant from
Dracula's thrall using the time-
honored method, in Horror of
Dracula, 1958.

Below and right: Christopher
Lee's gruesome demise in Horror
of Dracula, 1958. Neither
crucifixes nor sunlight agree with
vampires' constitutions.

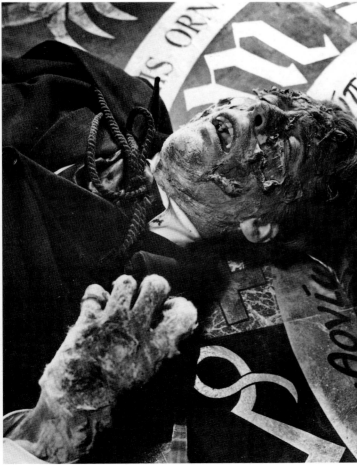

Apart from the fairly accurate resurrection of the Dracula of the 1890s, Hammer's *Dracula* (also called *Horror of Dracula*) was very much governed by contemporary constraints. The script-writer, Jimmy Sangster, was limited by budgetary dictates: costs had to be kept low. He therefore set Dracula's castle and the Holmwood residence within a short distance of each other, thereby eliminating the need for expensive portrayals of sea journeys and vampire chases across Europe. In addition, Stoker would have been appalled (as were the critics) by the Count's blatantly erotic appeal to his female victims (played by Melissa Stribling and Carol Marsh), whose bosoms heaved suggestively in delicious anticipation of Lee's sensual embrace. Beginning with Deane's play, each successive version of *Dracula* brought something new to vampire lore; Hammer, as a matter of policy, endowed the Count with charismatic sex appeal, offset by an emphasis on the bestial, ruthless nature of the vampire.

Regardless of the benefits of this somewhat dubious development, under Terence Fisher's direction, the heavy-handed treatment of the *Dracula* of 1931 was abandoned, and the 1958 model was transformed into a subtle and ironic social commentary, highlighting the degeneracy of the nineteenth century aristocracy, with its seductive appeal to the hypocritical, sexually repressed petty bourgeoisie. Poetic sequences throughout, and the final, gruesome shots of Lee, decomposing rapidly in the sun's rays, held audiences rapt, even if they offended the censors, who had already banned many scenes as being too shocking for public consumption.

By far the most superior Dracula film to date, *Horror of Dracula* was a triumph of production, and of casting. Peter Cushing, as the determined Van Helsing perfectly complemented what one critic called Lee's 'nineteenth century equivalent of James Bond.' While *The Curse of Frankenstein* had first established the two as an ideal foil for each other, *Horror of Dracula* would link the pair irrevocably in the public's minds. However, it would be over a decade before the two would act out the battle between good and evil again.

The part of Dracula's main antagonist is crucial to the Dracula story. A counterbalance to Dracula's evil supernatural power, Van Helsing represents the force of goodness: a human savior. The supporting casts of Dracula films are generally weak, peripheral characters: 'vampire-fodder.' Not so Van Helsing. His specialized knowledge ensures that it is he alone who can battle with the vampire on (nearly) equal terms. Furthermore, most humans (particularly women) lack the strong willpower required to resist Dracula's hypnotic powers. Van Helsing is the only one with enough self-control to do so, and even he nearly succumbs in the 1931 film. It is his lonely duty both to convince the sceptics of the seriousness of the vampire's threat and, armed with his unrivaled expertise and moral rectitude, to nullify the threat of his malevolent opponent.

Stoker's Van Helsing is represented as an eccentric boffin, an elderly, dry academic, whose imperfect command of the English language introduces an inadvertent element of comedy. However, he commands our respect because of his unparalleled understanding of the nature of the 'beast'. Edward Van Sloan's Van Helsing in the *Dracula* of 1931 was a stiff, somewhat dull, representation of the character. Cushing, however, brought life to the role. His charisma and athleticism made him a convincing rival to Lee's Dracula, particularly since the role requires a certain degree of violence, for while expertise is a powerful weapon, force is inevitably required to annihilate the vampire. In Cushing, Van Helsing at last appeared a hero in every sense of the word. In later films, however, the part of the anti-vampire hunter would frequently be given to younger, more romantic heroes, armed with little more than the power of love.

Not quite realizing the phenomenal extent of Lee's popularity in the role of Dracula, Hammer's next vampire film, *Brides of Dracula* ('Brides' referring to a harem of vampire women), released in 1960, did not feature Lee (or Count Dracula, for that matter), but the young, blond, blue-eyed David Peel as Baron Meister. To the movie-going public, the effect was not comparable. Although the film made a profit, it became clear to Hammer's executives that such was the feeling of nostalgia for Lee's performance in the role, that he must be tempted back.

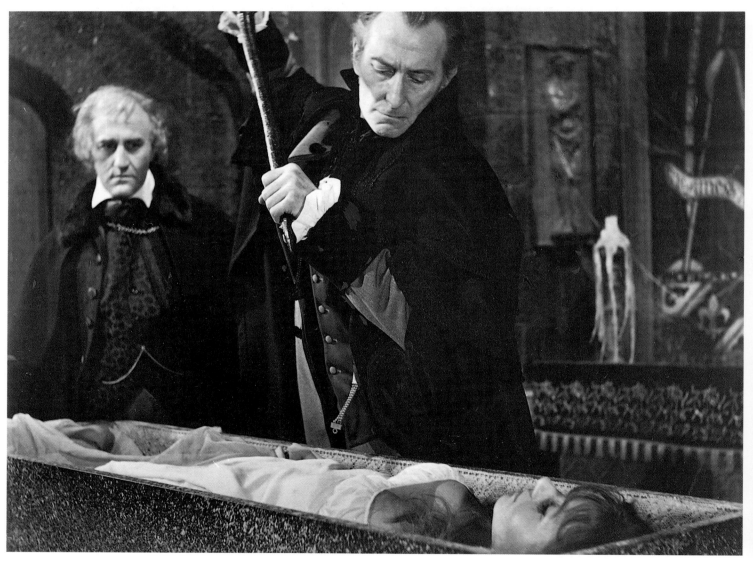

In the intervening years between *Horror of Dracula* and his next appearance as the Count, Lee had become a major 'horror' star, with films such as *The Mummy*, *The Hound of the Baskervilles* and *The Man Who Could ·Cheat Death*, under his belt. Although he consented to star in *Dracula, Prince of Darkness* in 1965, he had now become an expensive commodity, his services being charged on a daily rate. This consideration, perhaps, explains the fact that his scenes in the film are brief and largely silent.

The scriptwriter, again Jimmy Sangster (although the writing was credited to a fictitious 'John Sansom'), had the important difficulty of credibility to surmount. Much of the acclaim for *Horror of Dracula* came from the manner of Dracula's demise, his body dramatically crumbling away into dust. How could these particles be reassembled in such a way that the public would be convinced? Sangster's solution to this problem would be used time and time again: in later sequels Dracula was repeatedly revived, phoenix-like, by the dripping of freshly-drawn blood upon his powdery remains.

The plot of *Dracula, Prince of Darkness* was unimaginative; a

Left: *Christopher Lee's demise in icy waters in* Dracula, Prince of Darkness, *1965.*

Below and right: *You can't keep a good man down . . . Christopher Lee is resurrected, only to be despatched again in* Dracula Has Risen From The Grave, *1968.*

travelers' cautionary tale of the perils of using Dracula's castle as a hotel. However, under Terence Fisher's direction there were still some fine moments, particularly from Barbara Shelley as the vampirized Helen, culminating in Dracula's 'death' by drowning in the icy waters of the castle's moat. In an interesting departure from the Van Helsing angle, 'good' is represented by a religious agent: Father Sandor (Andrew Keir). Yet, despite the film's faults, box-office receipts justified the hiring of Lee, and the gift of a pair of fangs to each ticket-buyer also proved an added attraction.

By the late 1960s, the cult of youth and an increasingly permissive society had forced production companies to tailor their approach accordingly, in order to continue cashing in on their films. The horror genre did not escape this trend and, in the later *Dracula* films, we see the Count being pushed to the sidelines while the once peripheral inclusion of a love story comes to the fore.

The first of such films was *Dracula Has Risen From The Grave* (sometimes also titled *Dracula's Revenge*), released in 1968. Lee's role was subordinate to the main interest of the romantic relationship between a young student, Paul (Barry Edwards) and Maria (Veronica Carlson), upon whom Dracula has designs. The film again replaced Van Helsing with religious crusaders: a Monsignor (Maria's uncle), played by Rupert Davies, and a priest (Ewan Hooper). However, such is the power of Dracula, that when the priest unwittingly revives the Count with his blood, he becomes enslaved. Another development in vampire lore is Dracula's newly-found ability to survive the stake, unless prayers accompany impalement. Thus, since Paul is an atheist, his repeated attempts to finish Dracula off are ineffectual. It is only when Dracula is impaled upon a cross, thereby releasing the priest from his power in time to incant the necessary words, that Dracula is once again relegated to dust.

Left and right: Taste the Blood of Dracula, 1969, *saw Christopher Lee's magnetic power over women at its strongest.*

Below: Scars of Dracula (1970) *returned the Count to his mid-European homeland.*

Hammer's market research and massive advertising campaign had paid off. In financial terms, the film was the most successful Dracula project up to then, encouraging Hammer to commit itself to making annual sequels.

In 1969 *Taste the Blood of Dracula* returned Lee to Victorian England, a period to which he was best suited and which Peter Sasdy's direction skilfully enhanced. Lord Courtley (Ralph Bates), is the archetypal depraved English aristocrat and a dabbler in black magic. Courtley enlists the services of three outwardly stern and moral specimens of Victorian fatherhood. Secretly, however, eager for excitement, the trio have formed a 'society' for the furtherance of illicit practices, their hypocrisy and corruption illustrating the thin veneer of Victorian virtue. Having obtained Dracula's cloak, clasp and ring (Lee had taken to wearing a replica of Bela Lugosi's) and a phial containing the ashes, Courtley conjures up Dracula in a derelict church by mixing his own blood with the phial's contents and drinking this horrible brew. His three witnesses are appalled and kill Courtley before fleeing. A cocoon forms round Courtley's corpse, which splits to reveal Dracula. Determined to avenge the murder of his 'host', Dracula vampirizes the men's children and impels them to murder their fathers. Dracula is finally trapped in the church by a profusion of crucifixes and dies, crumbling into dust.

Unfortunately, from this time on, the quality of Dracula films suffered as budgets were further slashed and cheap sensationalism became more pronounced. *Scars of Dracula*, 1970 (featuring, among others, Dennis Waterman and Anoushka Hempel), brought little of value to the Dracula saga, apart from an interesting scene straight from Stoker's pen, in which Dracula crawls down the walls of his castle. Another novelty was the destruction of the Count by a bolt of lightning.

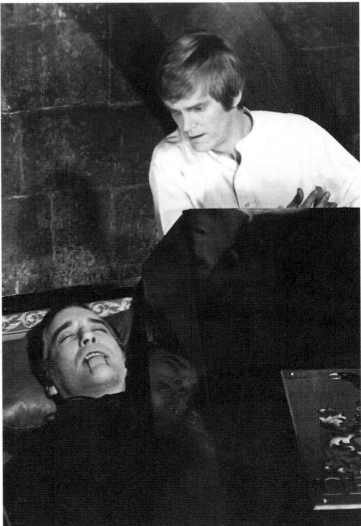

Under increasing pressure from the competition engendered by the profusion of steamy vampire films released by rival production companies, Hammer tried desperately to rekindle its earlier success, resorting to wilder and more ludicrous plots. *Dracula A.D. 1972*, although bringing back Peter Cushing as the grandson of the original Van Helsing (whose granddaughter, played by Stephanie Beacham is menaced by Dracula's bloodlust), was abysmal. Influenced by an American trend to contemporize the action, the film was set in swinging Chelsea and was a disastrous attempt to appeal to a teenage audience. The fact that it was also known as *Dracula Chases the Mini Girls* just about sums up the content and standard of the film.

Lee was becoming increasingly unhappy with Hammer's attempts to update the Dracula story and was well aware of his responsibility to his faithful fans:

> . . . people who go to see a character like this go to see him seriously. They don't laugh at him . . . In whatever context I play it, I don't change . . . whenever they do one of these things, they write the story first, then rack their brains to think of a way of inserting the main character into the framework of that story . . . this, of course, is ludicrous.

The Satanic Rites of Dracula (aka *Dracula is Alive and Well and Living in London*), released in 1972, was the last straw for Lee. A

These pages: Dracula AD 1972 *aka* Dracula Chases the Mini Girls *saw Christopher Lee in swinging London practising black magic among Chelsea teenagers. His demise, however, was of a strictly traditional nature. Unlike Dracula himself, who grows younger with every bloody meal, by the 1970s, Christopher Lee's Count was beginning to look a little older.*

simplistic analogy between bloodsucking and capitalism, Hammer cast Lee as a business tycoon and property developer, threatening to unleash bacteriological plague throughout the world. In the course of the film Van Helsing's (Peter Cushing) daughter (Joanna Lumley) is kidnapped, but eventually Dracula is, as always, foiled. His demise in a blazing hawthorn bush also spelt the end of Lee as Dracula, undoubtedly to his relief, since it was impossible for him to remain true to his self-imposed duty of portraying the character as Stoker had described him.

The only one of Lee's Dracula films which closely followed Stoker's *Dracula* was a Spanish, Italian and German production of 1970, *El Conde Dracula*, which also featured Klaus Kinski who would later star in the remake of *Nosferatu*. Although generally disappointing, Lee points out the importance of the film as a direct link to Dracula's creator: '. . . It is an old man in a black frockcoat, with white hair and a white moustache, getting progressively younger during the film as he gets stronger and stronger because of the blood. It is the only time . . . that Stoker's character has been presented authentically.'

Lee and Lugosi, in their heydays, had both been instrumental in ensuring Dracula's lasting appeal, and it is fitting that it should be these two actors who have become the most closely identified with the King Vampire. However, the role of Dracula has been tackled by many other actors who, while not as celebrated, have nevertheless brought something to the Dracula saga.

Left and below: *The final film in the Hammer Dracula series,* The Satanic Rites of Dracula, *1973,* climaxes dramatically with the burning of Christopher Lee's country mansion.

Right: El Conde Dracula, *1970,* gained Christopher Lee's approval as '... the only time ... that Stoker's character has been presented authentically.'

Overleaf: 'Welcome to my house! Enter freely and of your own will!' *Bela Lugosi invites a suspicious Dwight Frye into Castle Dracula,* Dracula, *1931.*

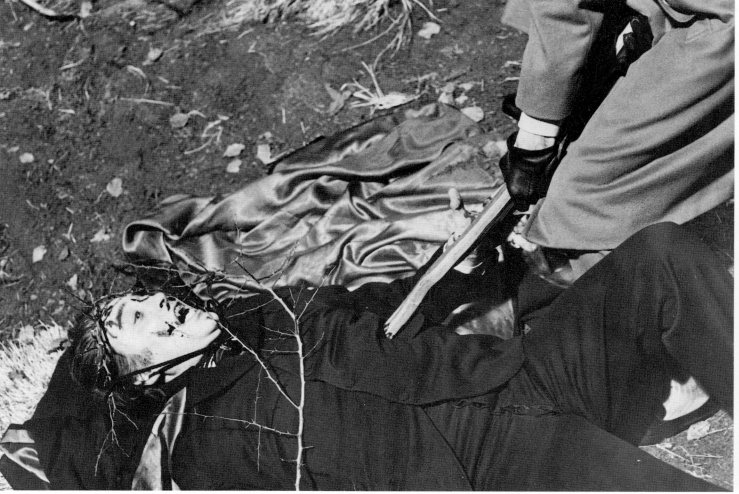

Various Vampires

'For centuries to come, he might, amongst its teeming millions . . .

create a new and ever-widening circle of semi-demons

to batten on the helpless.'

STOKER, *Dracula*

It has been the misfortune of the many talented actors who have taken on the role of Dracula, that they have not only faced the daunting challenge of bringing the Count to life, but also had the formidable specters of Lugosi and Lee to contend with.

The first major Hollywood star to grapple with Lugosi's legacy was Lon Chaney Jr., son of the famous horror actor. Fresh from his success in *The Wolf Man*, (1941), Universal reasoned that he would attract viewers and therefore cast him in the leading role of *Son of Dracula*, released in 1943. For reasons of financial expediency, Universal set the story entirely in America, a move justified by the Count himself in the script as having been necessary because of the unlimited supply of blood available to him in the New World. For the first time in the history of *Dracula* films, the vampire is given the name 'Count Alucard', which, as the movie's Professor Laslo (J Edward Bromberg) eventually deduces, is actually 'Dracula' spelt backwards. This nomenclature would be used many times again in later *Dracula* films.

The script has Chaney, safely ensconced in his coffin, arriving by train in the American deep south to fulfil his ghastly aim of seducing a southern belle (Louise Albritton) whom he first met in Transylvania. He succeeds in his goal, but finally meets his deserved end in the murky waters of a tunnel. Although *Son of Dracula* was distinguished by some startling photographic effects, particularly Chaney's metamorphosis into a vampire bat, Chaney himself seemed unsuited to the role of the Count. Thickset, and every inch American in appearance, his attempt to recreate Lugosi's smooth foreign nobleman is uncomfortable and unconvincing. Furthermore, Dracula just didn't seem as threatening when deprived of his Hungarian accent.

Left: *Lon Chaney Jr. and Louise Albritton in* Son of Dracula, *1943.*

Above: In Son of Dracula, *Lon Chaney Jr. stars as the mysterious Count Alucard, a stranger who turns up on a Southern plantation and has a habit of disappearing in puffs of smoke.*

In contrast, by abandoning Lugosi's style, John Carradine seemed to have found the key to challenging the public's loyalty to Lugosi. An erstwhile Shakespearian actor, Carradine had already impressed American audiences with his performances in films such as *The Grapes of Wrath* (1940). Because Lugosi was under contract to other studios at the time of the making of the sequel to *Frankenstein meets the Wolf Man* (1943), in which Lugosi had featured, Universal approached Carradine with the offer of the part of Dracula in *House of Frankenstein*. Carradine accepted, with the proviso that he be allowed to abandon Lugosi's black pompadour and revert to Stoker's description of the Count. His resultant neat moustache and aquiline profile made Dracula an elegant figure indeed; an image matched by Carradine's restrained, but beautifully delivered portrayal.

Released in 1945, *House of Frankenstein* was an obvious attempt by Universal to cash in on its stable of formula monsters by gathering them together in one reel of film. Thus, among others, Lon Chaney Jr. reappears as the Wolf Man, Boris Karloff is a mad professor, and Carradine is Dracula, all linked by an artfully contrived, if somewhat ludicrous, story line. Ridiculous it may have been, but *House of Frankenstein* is noteworthy if only on the basis of Carradine's outstanding performance. Its box office profits encouraged Universal, despite the difficulty of reincarnating its now extremely dead cast of monsters, to release *House of Dracula* later in 1945.

Dracula (Carradine), the Wolf Man (Chaney) and Frankenstein's Monster (Glenn Strange) were nonetheless duly reunited. Rather than give Dracula his now predictable *raison d'être* of remorselessly preying on the innocent, the scriptwriter, Edward Lowe, required the Count, now unhappy with his state of vampirism, to seek a cure from the benevolent Doctor Edelmann (Onslow Stevens). (This device to elicit the sympathy of the audience for the vampire had already been used in *Condemned to Live* (1935) and *Dracula's Daughter* (1936).) Interestingly, the doctor pronounces that Dracula's condition is caused by the existence of parasites in his bloodstream. However, Dracula's desire for a cure does not mean that he has automatically become a convert to goodness and, before he dissolves in the sun's rays, he manages to transfuse his blood into Edelmann, thus passing on the vampiric infection.

Carradine's performance was again impressive, but was not enough to make up for the film's glaring flaws, particularly of credibility, and the audience's increasing weariness with this type of film. *House of Dracula* spelled the end of Universal's serious attempts to scare the movie-goers with the King Vampire. Carradine would return to play Dracula in other productions, including the Mexican film *Las Vampiras* (1967), and the appalling 'horror-disco-comedy' *Nocturna* (1979), but never again with as much success.

Left: *The wolf man meets the vampire; Matt Willis and Bela Lugosi in* The Return of the Vampire, *1944.*

Above: *The visually stunning climax to* The Return of Dracula, 1958, *starring Francis Lederer.*

The intervening years between *House of Dracula* and Lee's *Dracula* of 1958 were a vacuum, as far as the Count and his fans were concerned. There was one commendable portrayal of Dracula, however, which appeared on cinema screens in the same year as Lee's magnificent debut in the role, the latter thus totally overshadowing *The Return of Dracula*. This Gramercy film starred the Czech actor, Francis Lederer, and used a similar plot to that of *Son of Dracula*. Dracula (Lederer) arrives by train in California, having murdered a young artist en route in order to assume his identity. He is accepted by the artist's family and manages to vampirize two young girls before he is impaled on a densely packed bed of spikes lining the bottom of a deep pit. The refreshing aspect which Lederer brought to the role was that of total contemporariness: the curly-haired actor wore neither fangs nor evening wear, but was dressed instead in a 1950s' suit, overcoat and hat, thus injecting the flavor of a cold war spy into the part.

From 1958 until the early 1970s, Hammer had a virtual monopoly of *Dracula* movies and there was little room for any significant challenger to Lee's supremacy in the eyes of Western Dracula fans. Oriental movie-makers were less intimidated by the Lee/Hammer partnership and, in 1971, *Chi O Suu Me* (*Bloodthirty Eyes*) was released, featuring the first Japanese Dracula, in the shape of actor Mori Kishida. Sporting an awesome pair of fangs, flashing golden eyes and purportedly the descendent of Count Dracula and a Japanese woman, Kishida represented an interesting variation on the vampire theme. Unsurprisingly, though, he was never going to be a real contender for Lee's undisputed crown.

In total antithesis was German director Werner Herzog's tribute to Murnau, *Nosferatu: Phantom der Nacht* (*Nosferatu: Phantom of the Night*), also released in 1979. Herzog had long considered *Nosferatu: Eine Symphonie des Grauens* the most important film ever made in Germany, and in his zeal of unqualified admiration, proceeded literally to duplicate this 1920s' classic. Klaus Kinski, as the modern Nosferatu, could not have been more different to Langella's Dracula. Bald, with pointed ears and talon-like hands, Kinski's stark white face contrasted hideously with his red-rimmed eyes. Like Max Schreck before him, his elongated fangs were those of the rodent, rather than the canine. Isabelle Adjani played his luminous and enthralled victim, helpless against his supernatural hold. In many areas the film came unintentionally close to parody, but the total effect, enhanced by some breathtakingly haunting camerawork, is one of great artistry.

Left: *Francis Lederer awakes in* The Return of Dracula, 1958, *a film totally overshadowed by the release in the same year of* Hammer's Horror of Dracula.

Right: *William Marshall goes in for the kill in* Blacula, 1972.

Below: *Louis Jourdan starred in Philip Savill's made-for-television production,* Count Dracula, 1978.

By the end of the 1970s, television was threatening the cinema as the main medium for popular escapism. Television sets were becoming ubiquitous, and the public was fast realizing the benefits of having their own in-house mini cinema. It was inevitable that Dracula would appear on TV and, indeed, in 1956 Carradine played the Count in *Matinée Theatre*; later – in 1970 – Denholm Elliott starred in a BBC production. The definitive TV Dracula, however, was Jack Palance, who assumed the role in Dan Curtis Productions/Universal's TV show of 1973.

The scriptwriter, Richard Matheson, modeled the story as closely as possible on Stoker's book (hence the film's alternative title *Bram Stoker's Dracula*). Unlike other films, this version stressed Dracula's previous existence as Vlad the Impaler, and Matheson mixed a certain pathos with the love interest, since Dracula is mesmerized by Lucy Westernra's (Fiona Lewis) exact resemblance to his fifteenth century sweetheart, Maria. Palance made an ideal Dracula: his clean-shaven and distinguished appearance perfectly complemented by his impressive acting ability.

One further 'straight' Dracula film should be mentioned: Mirisch/Universal's *Dracula* of 1979. This production, based on Deane's play, was a lush, stylish, almost camp affair, including some spectacular special effects. The film features Laurence Olivier, but the real star was Dracula himself, played by Frank Langella. Langella's Dracula cut a dashing, youthful and romantic figure (and, incidentally, bore a startling resemblance to John Travolta, the disco-dancing star of *Saturday Night Fever*). However, Dracula as a matinée idol, although going down well with the female viewers, was not an image that the Dracula purists happily accepted.

Below and left: *Dracula as a matinée idol – Frank Langella in Dracula, 1979. One critic praised the stylishness of the movie, but also said it steered 'between the reefs of camp and theatrical indulgence.'*

Right: *Werner Herzog's Nosferatu of 1979 starring the late Klaus Kinski, was a faithful reworking of Murnau's classic of the 1920s.*

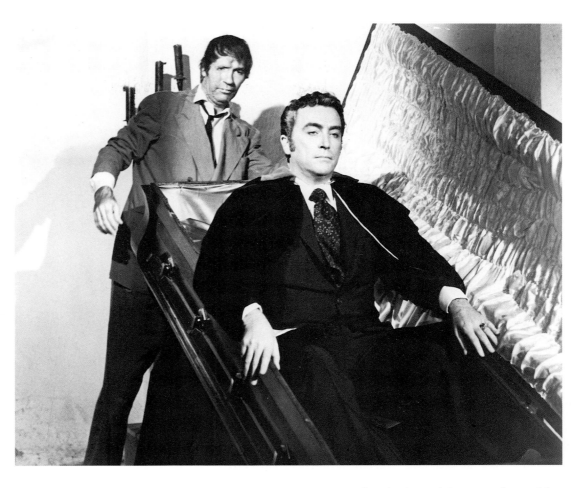

Left and right: *Robert Quarry,
alias 'Count Yorga', starred in two
films during the early 1970s and
took the vampire's threat to
contemporary Los Angeles.*

The Dracula story has not been immune from sometimes drastic adaptation by film companies, trying to cash in on their carefully selected target audiences. The most notable of these attempts is American International's *Blacula* of 1972. This blatant move to harness the militant feeling of black pride which was sweeping America in the wake of the civil rights struggle was not the first example of 'blaxploitation', nor would it be the last.

Sadly, the script misses the opportunity to make intelligent use of its black focus. The only social comment passed is in the prologue, when Mamuwalde, a black African prince (played by the Shakespearian actor, William Marshall), visits Count Dracula (Charles Macaulay) in nineteenth-century Transylvania to try to persuade him to help halt the trade in black slaves. This contrived angle was Marshall's suggestion, and was included against the better judgement of the studio; it certainly strikes an incongruous note. The rest of the story follows a by now routine pattern: Dracula turns out to be racist, vampirizes Mamuwalde and seals him in a coffin to die. The scene switches to the 1970s: the contents of Dracula's castle, including Blacula's coffin, are shipped to Los Angeles by the American buyers, where Blacula is revived. Having stalked the streets of Los Angeles, and vampirized its citizens, Blacula is finally tracked down by the police and voluntarily exposes himself to the sun's deadly rays.

It was, perhaps, inevitable that Blacula would not be allowed to rest in peace, but was resurrected in 1973 to appear in *Scream Blacula Scream*. This time Marshall was required to become entangled with a voodoo cult and his eventual death was by proxy: with an impaled voodoo doll.

One curious and unique version of Dracula was aimed at a different minority group: the deaf. *Deafula* was released by Signscope in 1975 and starred Peter Wechsburg, also the director and scriptwriter, as 'Deafula.' The film is conducted in deaf-and-dumb sign language throughout.

It was becoming painfully clear to the movie-makers of the 1970s that Dracula was in danger of becoming a victim of audience fatigue. There had been so many Dracula films that it was becoming almost impossible for the Dracula industry to retain the public's enthusiasm for the character. The studios thus faced a real dilemma: Dracula's appeal seemed to have been milked dry; every conceivable novelty within the constraints of Stoker's tale had already been tried, and yet the studios believed that there was still financial capital to be made from vampires. But how to do it?

One solution was to give Dracula a new identity: Count Yorga, for example. Erica Productions/American International took this angle in 1970, with the release of *Count Yorga, Vampire*. Based in contemporary America, Count Yorga (Robert Quarry) is, to all intents and purposes, Count Dracula by another name, and the film follows traditional Dracula lines. The evil count holds seances as a means of mesmerizing and then vampirizing beautiful women, but is finally thwarted by a brave boyfriend and a suspicious doctor. The sequel, *The Return of Count Yorga* (1971), followed similar lines. Vampire films were now increasingly being set in contemporary locations, thus bringing the threat closer to the audience. *Salem's Lot* (1979), the television version of Stephen King's novel, had David Soul menaced by Reggie Nalder's vampire in Maine, while *The Hunger* (1983), an adaptation of Whitley Strieber's novel, saw Catherine Deneuve and David Bowie terrorizing fashionable nightclubs.

An alternative option was the double gimmick of using Dracula's name in the film's title, but giving the starring role of villain not to the Count, but to . . . a dog. *Dracula's Dog* was accordingly released by VIC in 1977. The coffins of the Dracula household are disturbed in Romania and are promptly burned, all except two, whose occupants are missing. These two are a hideous being grandiloquently described as a 'fractional lamia' – a non-vampire – (played by Reggie Nalder), who was Count Dracula's servant; and Zoltan, Dracula's vampiric dog. Both creatures yearn for a master and therefore set sail for Los Angeles, where the last (unvampirized) scion of the Dracula line is living, under a different name, blissfully ignorant of his ancestry. Zoltan succeeds in vampirizing a number of unfortunate canines, but fails to recruit his intended master.

Yet another variation on the theme, and by far the most successful, was Dracula's female equivalent. This was not an entirely new concept: Gloria Holden had starred, to great acclaim, in *Dracula's Daughter* in 1936. *Dracula's Daughter* was Universal's first sequel to its *Dracula* of 1931 and it picks up the story at the exact point where *Dracula* finished.

Above: Klaus Kinski sporting an incredible pair of bat-like ears, prepares to vampirize Isabelle Adjani in Nosferatu, 1979.

Right: Klaus Kinski's vampire was closely modeled on Max Schreck's prototype, including the rodent-like canines. Isabelle Adjani's luminous heroine provided the perfect contrast.

The police arrive at Carfax Abbey and arrest van Helsing (Edward van Sloan) for the murders of Renfield and Count Dracula, since they are unaware of Dracula's true identity. The corpses are removed to a morgue and are placed under guard. However, during the night watch, a lovely dark-haired woman, clothed in black, appears and hypnotizes the lone police constable, sending him into a trance with her mysteriously mesmerizing ring. She then removes Dracula's corpse to a lonely forest and proceeds to cremate it, holding a crucifix aloft (with considerable distaste) while chanting an exorcism to free his soul. This is Dracula's daughter, alias Countess Marya Zaleska (Gloria Holden). It transpires that she had hoped Dracula's death would free her from her unnatural cravings, but this has not happened; she is miserable with her vampiric state and wishes to be freed. On consulting the sympathetic Doctor Garth (Otto Kruger), she is advised that her problem is psychological and that she must confront it in order to re-

solve it. Accordingly, she has her sinister manservant, Sandor (Irving Pichel), kidnap a young model so that she can test her willpower, but she is unable to resist the temptation to vampirize her. Recognizing that she will always remain a vampire, she tries to persuade the increasingly suspicious Garth, with whom she has fallen in love, to return to Transylvania with her. When he refuses, she forces the issue by seizing his fiancée, Janet Blake (Marguerite Churchill) and spiriting her away to her homeland. Van Helsing and Garth give chase and, on their arrival at Dracula's castle, Garth is blackmailed into agreeing to suffer the Countess's bite. On the verge of vampirization, he is saved by the Countess from a deadly arrow, fired by the jealous Sandor who, about to see the gift of immortality which the Countess had promised him snatched away and bestowed upon another, must resort to the most final means to prevent this betrayal. Staked by the arrow's wooden shaft, the Countess finds release from her torment.

Left: *David Bowie mesmerizes Ann Magnusson in* The Hunger, *1983.*

Right and below: *Zoltan, canine star of* Dracula's Dog, *1977. Zoltan is used by Dracula's resurrected servant in an attempt to recreate a new master.*

Overleaf: *Universal's suitably lurid promotional poster for* Son of Dracula, *1943.*

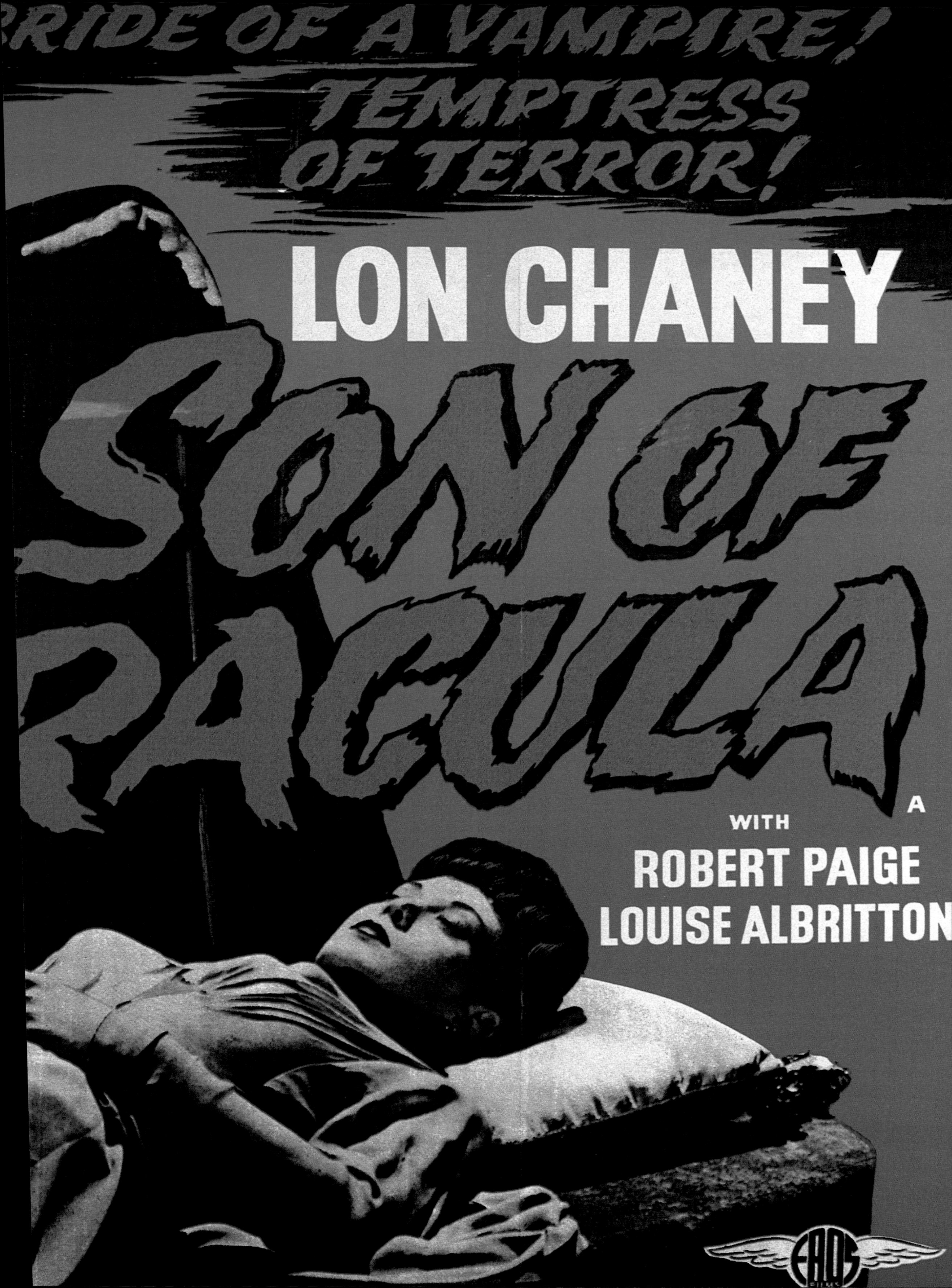
BRIDE OF A VAMPIRE!
TEMPTRESS OF TERROR!
LON CHANEY
SON OF DRACULA
A
WITH
ROBERT PAIGE
LOUISE ALBRITTON

Left: *Gloria Holden, as Countess Marya Zaleska and her devoted servant, Irving Pichel, Dracula's Daughter, 1936.*

Below left: *The incomparable Gloria Holden, in an atmospheric scene from Dracula's Daughter, 1936.*

Right: *Staked by an arrow, Gloria Holden dies in the arms of the man she loves, Otto Kruger.*

Below right: *Elisabeth Bathory, the 'Blood Countess' of Transylvania, and the historical figure on whom the frightening female vampires were based.*

Dracula's Daughter was a much underrated film: low-key and sensitively shot, it is a marvelous and tasteful prototype of the female vampire film. Gloria Holden's Countess was a truly tragic figure, in the classical Greek tradition, while her acting skills and great beauty elicited simultaneous sympathy and revulsion.

Not so the next movie centering on a female bloodsucker, released in 1957. The title, *Blood of Dracula*, is a total misnomer, for neither Dracula nor his blood feature in the story. Nancy Perkins (Sandra Harrison), the most unpopular girl in school, is hypnotized by a medallion (which might have belonged to Dracula) wielded by the unsavory chemistry teacher (Louise Lewis). She consequently becomes a vampire and periodically terrorizes the school before being impaled. *Blood of Dracula* was one of a string of films directed at the teenage market, which now made up a significant proportion of movie-goers and, as such, has limited appeal to adult viewers. Sandra Harrison, however, made an alarming female vampire; her college-girl clothing contrastingly grotesquely with her appearance when in the grip of bloodlust. Enormous, unruly eyebrows and bushy black hair springing from a widow's peak, uneven fangs and a chalky-white, almost masculine face, ensured that Sandra Harrison, in full make-up, was not a pretty sight.

The studios had not just plucked the concept of a female equivalent of Count Dracula from the air. Just as Stoker's *Dracula* had been based upon a verifiable historical figure, so 'Countess Dracula' had a real sixteenth-century antecedent: Countess Elizabeth Bathory.

Born in Transylvania in 1560, the 'Blood Countess', as she came to be known, married Count Ferencz Nasady at the age of fifteen. Her husband preferred warfare to a sedentary life at their castle at Csejthe, and it was during his prolonged absences that Elizabeth indulged her unappetizing interests of lesbianism, witchcraft, sadism and vampirism. It was not long before her depraved dabblings became an obsession, and Elizabeth and her cronies started to capture young servant girls from the neighboring village, imprisoning and torturing them. As her remarkable beauty faded with age, Elizabeth, who was excessively vain, became increasingly desperate to regain her youth and was, therefore, delighted when her chief witch, Darvulia, informed her that she could reverse the ravages of time by bathing in the blood of virgins. It was estimated by contemporary sources that at least 650 young women, servant girls and noblewomen alike, died at the orders of the Countess, before she was finally brought to justice in 1610. She was tried, judged to be criminally insane, and was walled up within her fortress until her death four years later. This story, along with Le Fanu's *Carmilla*, may have provided some of the inspiration for Stoker's omitted *Dracula* chapter, *Dracula's Guest*. However, it was not until the 1970s that the Blood Countess was 'discovered' by movie-makers.

In 1970, the same year as it released *Scars of Dracula*, Hammer unleashed *Countess Dracula* on to cinema screens. Although the film was based upon the life of Elizabeth Bathory, Hammer judged it expedient, for commercial reasons, to link Bathory with Dracula and did so, via the title. The ageing Countess was played by Ingrid Pitt, who would also star in *The Vampire Lovers* that same year. Pitt had cornered the market in the portrayal of female vampires, with justification, for she was frequently called upon to interpret particularly demanding parts and did so with consummate skill.

Above: Ingrid Pitt, *the ruthless and unsavory* Countess Dracula, 1970. *Bathing in blood countless times for the purposes of cinema, Ingrid Pitt held the monopoly in portraying female vampires in the 1970s.*

Right: Hammer's Kiss of the Vampire, *released in 1962 was a chilling triumph for its director, Don Sharp.*

Countess Dracula, directed by Peter Sasdy, required Pitt to transform herself from wrinkled harridan to nubile girl, rejuvenated by the blood of young virgins. Envious of her daughter's (Lesley-Anne Down) personal attractions and lack of years, she incarcerates her and assumes her identity, in order to fascinate a dashing hussar (Sandor Eles), and dupes him into a proposing marriage. Unfortunately for the Countess, the effects of her bloodbaths cease during the wedding ceremony, revealing her actual hideous, withered self She slashes at her daughter, who has been released to witness the happy occasion but, instead of receiving a shower of invigorating blood, only succeeds in killing her bridegroom The final, poignant scene shows her gazing into a mirror, awaiting her execution. *Countess Dracula* remains the most important example of the Countess Bathory film genre, the sole serious challenger to Pitt being Lucia Bose in the Spanish film *Ceremonia Sangrienta* (1972).

Even though the female vampire was a diverting alternative to Count Dracula, she never really captured the public's imagination to quite the same extent, at least not when she represented merely a straight transposition of gender. It seemed that vampirism would have to be divorced completely from the Dracula persona if it was to be the subject of more innovative and inventive treatment. A flood of such non-Dracula vampire movies therefore swamped the cinemas of the 1970s, many of which were quite dreadful, in questionable taste and abysmally executed. However, there were a few examples of this trend which stood out from the rest.

Hammer's early offering, *Kiss of the Vampire* (1962), featuring Noel Willman as a Ravna, a noble nineteenth-century Bavarian vampire, was one such quality movie. The film incorporated many characteristics traditional to *Dracula* films, such as the puritanical Professor Zimmer (Clifford Evans) as the 'white knight' crusading against Ravna's vampiric orgies, and the near-corruption of a young bride (Jennifer Daniel); but it still manages to steer clear of the Dracula-by-another-name syndrome. There are also some deeply sinister and frightening moments, including the final scene, in which a swarm of bats close in on and attack Ravna's entrapped disciples of vampirism.

Like *Kiss of the Vampire*, Roman Polanski's *Dance of the Vampires* (Cadre Films/Filmways), released in 1967, borrowed heavily from bona fide Dracula movies. This brilliant oeuvre defies classification as either 'horror' or 'spoof', incorporating both elements to produce a magnificent black comedy. Count Von Krolock (Ferdy Mayne) kidnaps Sarah (Sharon Tate), the delectable daughter of an innkeeper, and bears her off to his Transylvanian castle. It falls to Professor Ambrosius (Jack MacGowran) and his assistant Alfred (Polanski) to rescue Sarah from the Count's evil clutches. Evading the amorous attentions of Von Krolock's homosexual son (Iain Quarrier), Alfred, along with the Professor, manage to abduct Sarah from a bizarre vampire social event – a dance – and make their escape from the assembled guests in a sleigh. It is too late, however, both for Sarah, and for Alfred, for she bares her newly-sprouted fangs and bites him.

Left: *Ingrid Pitt, flanked by faithful servant, Nigel Green, in* Countess Dracula, *1970.*

Above: *A gory scene from* Vampire Circus, *which recounted the bizarre tale of a plague-ridden village invaded by animal vampires.*

Right: *Roman Polanski and Sharon Tate in the superb* Dance of the Vampires.

The comic touches in *Dance of the Vampires* are superlative, none better than when a Jewish vampire laughs off an attempt to ward him off with a crucifix, yet the moments of horror are quite chilling. There was a sour postscript to this film, which was released in America under two titles: *The Fearless Vampire Killers* and, unforgivably, *Pardon Me But Your Teeth Are In My Neck*. Polanski was understandably upset by this supposedly witty trivialization and demanded the removal of his name from the credits.

Vampire Circus (Hammer, 1971) was an ingenious move away from the strictures of the standard vampire film, although it incorporated both a count and castle. In 1825, a remote Serbian village is striken by the plague, a scourge which coincides with the visit of the itinerant 'Circus of the Nights.' The circus troupe is, in fact, a band of vampires and their first action is the revival of the village's own deceased vampire, Count Mitterhouse (Robert Taymann), by means of the blood of the Bürgermeister's daughter. Using their supernatural powers to transform themselves into animals (splendidly filmed), they entrap their admiring victims in a maze of mirrors as a prelude to vampirization. It seems as though the leaders of the troupe (Adrienne Corri and Anthony Corlan) will bleed the already severely depleted villagers dry. The vampires are doomed, however, when the remaining villagers bravely encircle them with a ring of fire. In the earlier scenes, the film had showed great promise, but its initial potential was spoiled by an over-enthusiasm for sex scenes (many of which were cut by the censor), thus further disrupting the tenuous thread of continuity running through this bizarre, but inventive movie.

An entirely different treatment of the vampire was taken by Braddock Associates in their harrowing production *Martin*, released in 1976. Martin (John Amplas) is a wholesome-looking Pittsburgh teenager, who also happens to be an ancient, evil vampire, preying upon Pittsburgh's complacent suburban citizens. The unnerving aspect of this film is that the age-old weapons against vampirism – garlic and exorcism – no longer have any effect upon this contemporary vampire. Indeed, Martin makes fun of popular vampire lore, in one scene even prancing through the streets kitted out in full Lugosi gear and false fangs. *Martin* highlights the disturbing paradox between modern-day scepticism and traditional superstitions and, by playing on our paranoia, leaves the viewer uneasy and troubled.

The classic *Dracula* had spawned a new family of hybrids within the horror genre, the mutant vampires reaching their apogee in the 1970s as movie-makers catered for the public's apparently insatiable desire to be scared by vampires, either of the Dracula variety or otherwise. After the 1970s, however, the public's fickle allegiance switched away from the traditional monsters towards the more gory thrills of science fiction and gruesome 'psychological' horror movies. Vampire films were forced to take a back seat to these increasingly sophisticated horrors, but such is their unearthly fascination that, although temporarily out of the limelight, they are still being made and have retained their power to terrify.

Left: *The no-so innocent, and unspeakably bloodthirsty John Amplas in* Martin, 1976.

Right: A *scene from* Andy Warhol's Dracula, 1973, *directed by Antonio Margheriti, starring Udo Kier and featuring Roman Polanski.*

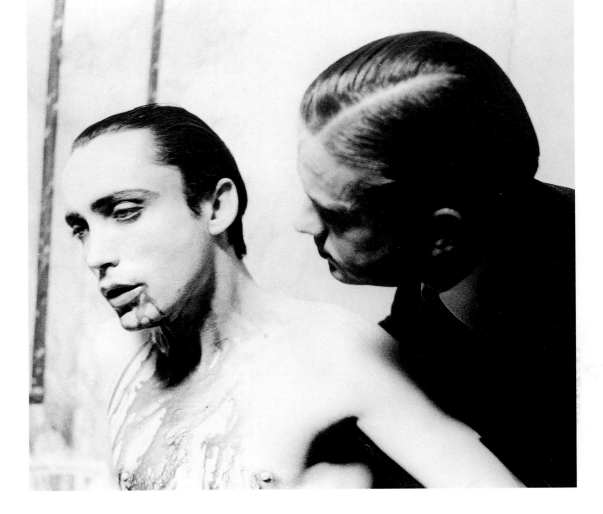

Dracula: Love, Sex, and Spoofs

'Have you felt the vampire's lips upon your throat?'

STOKER, *Dracula*

The primary purpose of horror films is to frighten: to send their audiences on a hair-raising roller coaster ride of terror. These collective nightmares, however, nearly always include a subplot – frequently a love story – intended both to capture the viewers' imagination, and to provide temporary relief from otherwise relentless scenes of horror. Indeed, where would any film be without its romantic interest? A good love story has universal appeal and can always be relied upon to boost the ratings. Movie-makers had always been aware of the importance of the suggestion of love in their Dracula films, which they regarded as necessary to elicit the public's interest still further, should the attractions of a 'straight' horror film begin to flag. Thus, promotional literature for the *Dracula* film of 1931 promised 'the strangest love story of all' and *Dracula* of 1958 was intriguingly described as 'the terrifying lover who died, yet lived.'

A more subtle approach was the presentation of Dracula scripts as beauty-and-the-beast stories, a concept calculated to play on movie-goers' empathy with the underdog. The emphasis is placed on the profound pathos of the central character's situation: unloved and unlovely, tormented by a hopeless and unrequited yearning to possess the unattainable object of his desire. The pathetic, hounded, love-lorn vampire is a powerfully moving image, but studios had to be careful not to overstress this dimension, for fear of turning their films which, after all, sold cinema tickets on their horror credentials, into poignant love stories. *Dracula's Daughter* is one such example: a vampiress who wishes to be human, falling in love with a mortal man. This film balances the schizophrenic conflict between good and evil well, for while the vampiress is intellectually unhappy with her situation, she is

Left: *Michael Johnson, in* Hammer's Lust for a Vampire, *1970. In this movie, a reincarnated vampire turns up in a mid-European girls school in 1830 – an unusual but entirely sensible choice of venue for a thirsty vampire.*

Above: *A dramatic scene from* Lust for a Vampire, *1970 – villagers and priest unite against the evil of the vampire.*

69

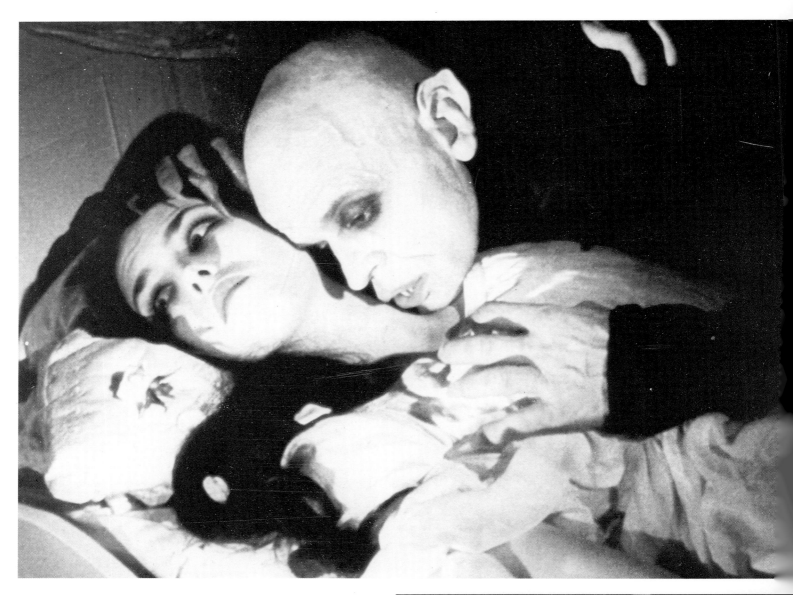

governed by baser, physical cravings (the horror element) which she cannot overcome until her final suicidal sacrifice to save her love's life (the love angle). Ultimately, however, the viewers are left in no doubt that the film is chiefly concerned with the threat of vampirism.

The attractiveness of the vampire has always been a crucial component of the overall success of Dracula films. Unlike many movie monsters, such as Frankenstein's, the vampire is, externally at least, human. Giving Dracula a human body, conventional clothing, fluent linguistic ability and courteous social graces contrives to make the threat to us far more subtle and sinister than if we were confronted with an alien being to whom we cannot relate. Dracula's danger, therefore, lies as much in our confused and insecure psychological reaction to his apparent 'normality', as in our more tangible fear of vampirism. Our fear becomes increasingly paranoid when, as in many 1970s' films, the vampire is removed from his Victorian setting and placed in our own time. The success of the vampire's threat is closely connected with his personal magnetism; the more good-looking and suave he is, the more we not only find ourselves able to empathize with him, but are attracted to him, half forgetting his real evil and twisted nature.

Furthermore, the menace of vampirism itself is closely

Left: *The vampire's embrace: Isabelle Adjani and Klaus Kinski in* Nosferatu *(1979); and* below left: *Veronica Carlson and Christopher Lee, in* Dracula has Risen from the Grave, *1968.*

Below: *Bela Lugosi with Helen Chandler who was the first to succumb to the charms of cinema's classic Dracula in 1931.*

linked to the sometimes destructive power of human sexuality. The act of vampirism is in itself ambiguous. Although we know that the life blood is being sucked from the victim's throat, the deadly method of blood-letting has all the outward signs of a passionate embrace. The post-vampirization behavior of the female victims of Dracula's blood lust compounds this ambiguity. They are frequently shown awaiting Dracula's bite reclining languidly in bed, as if expecting a lover. Once they have received his attentions, they become completely subservient to their 'master', devoted and submissive, just as if they had fallen in love. Yet, in other respects they become totally uninhibited, as if released from the repression of sexual convention. Barbara Shelley, for example, vampirized by Christopher Lee in *Dracula, Prince of Darkness* (1965), undergoes a startling transformation from sour, uptight frump to wild, voluptuous siren. Lugosi had his own theory explaining Dracula's fascination: 'It is women who love horror. They hoped that I was Dracula. They hoped that my love was the love of Dracula. It is the embrace of Death their subconscious is yearning for. Death, the final triumphant lover.'

Stoker himself had indicated the havoc which the disruptive sexual connotations associated with vampirism could play with the established social order. His female victims are stereotypical ideals of Victorian womanhood. On the one hand we have Lucy, who is innocent, appealing and weak, and pays for her submission with death; on the other Mina, the devoted wife who, while in possession of a strong will, common sense and Christian resolve, is nevertheless in danger of completely surrendering herself to Dracula. The inference is that women are too weak-willed to be able to resist the vampire's lure: they need to be 'saved from themselves' (as much as from Dracula's lust) by heroic men who are both morally and physically stronger.

Left: *Christopher Lee resists the charms of Jenny Hanley in* Scars of Dracula, *1970.*

Above: *Blonde, buxom and beautiful, Ingrid Pitt stars as the evil vampiress, Mircalla Karnstein, in* The Vampire Lovers, *1970.*

Thus, the most enduring depiction of females in Dracula films is that of the passive prey, powerless to resist Dracula's vampiric advances. Helen Chandler was the first pliant recipient of Bela Lugosi's dishonorable attentions in 1931, while Christopher Lee had his pick of a varied harem of ravishing young girls to vampirize in his many incarnations as Dracula.

As successive generations became more sophisticated in their requirements of Dracula movies, so the female roles became meatier and increasingly demanding. The concept of the predatory female vampire – the complete opposite to the vulnerable victim – presented a more palpable threat, which increased in direct proportion to the vampire's physical attractiveness. Sandra Harrison, in 1957's *Blood of Dracula* was a repellent figure in vampire guise, and her graphically hideous looks, while inducing a shudder of disgust, ultimately counted against her success in the league table of female vampires.

Again, Stoker had originally acknowledged the dangerous power inherent in a beautiful lady vampire, in his warning relayed through the idiosyncratic phraseology of Van Helsing:

> . . . the mere beauty and fascination of the wanton Un-Dead have hypnotise him and he remains on and on until sunset come and the vampire sleep be over. Then the beautiful eyes of the fair woman open and look love and the voluptuous mouth present to kiss – and man is weak. And there remains one more victim in the vampire fold, one more to swell the grim and grisly ranks of the Un-Dead.

What Stoker is describing is, in effect, the ultimate, man-eating 'vamp' (and, indeed, in 1986 Grace Jones was to star in a vampire film of this name); the alluring temptress who sends out messages of promise in order to ensnare her willing victim and then, once entrapped, despatches him without mercy (behavior reminiscent of the black widow spider). The seductive, yet deadly huntress, siren and emasculator – what a psychologically confusing and terrifying image (particularly for men) – and how well it translated on to cinema screens.

Hammer's *Twins of Evil* of 1971 (the third of the 'Karnstein trilogy', after *The Vampire Lovers* and *Lust for a Vampire*), neatly encapsulates the dual depiction of women in vampire films. The twins of the title were real-life twins, Mary and Madeleine Collinson, who played a pair of luscious beauties, fought over by Peter Cushing, as the austere Weil (a Van Helsing figure), and Damien Thomas as the evil vampire, Count Karnstein. The forces of puritanism and hedonistic excess each claim a twin: one is vampirized and is eventually despatched by decapitation, the other remains pure and is rescued by a handsome savior, while Weil and Karnstein, as representatives of the two moral extremes, finally destroy each other. Quite apart from these intriguing allegories, the film was also exceedingly well filmed and directed by John Hough.

It was inevitable that the potent possibilities of the corrupt beauty would be picked up upon with alacrity and exploited shamelessly by film studios, especially in the heady, liberated days of the 1960s and 1970s. In the 1970s, female vampires terrorized cinema audiences. Their dominance in these years can be explained by the liberalization of censorship on the one hand, and by the movie-makers' desire to find a new slant on the standard Dracula formula on the other hand. This was also the era of militant 'women's lib', a time when feminist issues were being aggressively pushed to the forefront, thus destabilizing the traditional male/female socio-sexual status quo. The result was a plethora of films in which armies of

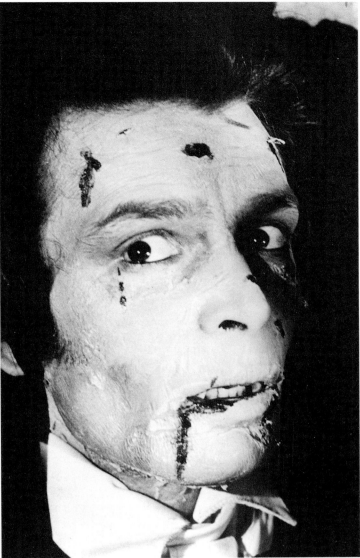

Left: *Christopher Lee sandwiched between two adoring victims in* Taste the Blood of Dracula, 1969.

Above: *An untypically tender moment from* The Vampire Lovers, 1970.

Above right: *Damien Thomas, as Count Karnstein, comes to a sticky end in* Twins of Evil, 1971.

menacing female vampires stalked, seduced and killed their helpless prey – both male and female – their physical attractiveness and rampant sexual exploits simultaneously threatening the predominantly male audience, yet also indulging its fantasies.

The danger was, that in their eagerness to attract droves of movie-goers to the cinema, film companies might go too far and spoil the 'vamp's' mysterious fascination by the overuse of gratuitous sex scenes and poor plots. There were far too many vampire films made in the 1960s and 1970s to catalogue them all here, suffice it to say that the general trend was towards lurid erotica. The alternative title of Jean Rollin's *Requiem pour un Vampire, Sex Vampires* (1971), sums up the downward direction in which vampire films were moving.

A typically uninspiring early example was made at the start of the 1960s: the Italian production, *L'amante del Vampiro* (*The Vampire's Lover*). The objects of desire are two young ballerinas (Helene Remy and Tina Gloriani), forced by inclement weather to request shelter in the castle of a vampiric Contessa (Maria Luisa Rolando) and her equally vampiric servant (Walter Brandi). Predictably, the dancers are duly exsanguinated and the vampires themselves finally crumble away on exposure to sunlight. The sole arresting idea given expression in the film is in the form of transferred vampirism: it is the ser-

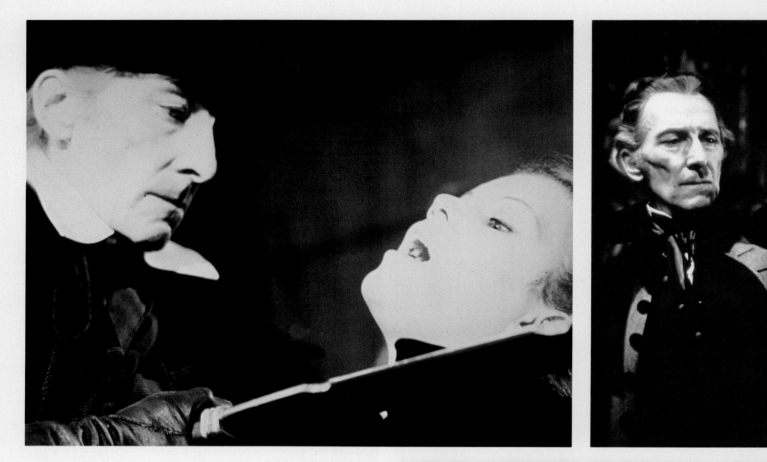

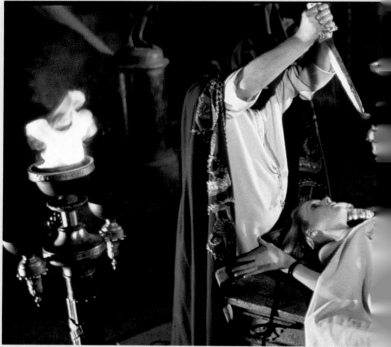

vant who vampirizes the ballerinas, after which he presents his own neck to the Contessa, so that she, in turn, may satiate her blood lust via him. Apart from this novelty, the film is of a low quality and comes perilously close to 'sexploitation'. A successor to this film, L'*Ultima Preda del Vampiro* (*The Last Victim of the Vampire*), again featuring Walter Brandi in the schizophrenic role of (good) Count Kernassy and his (evil) vampiric ancestor, continued in a similar vein, with numerous lingering close-ups of beautiful unclothed women, in particular of Maria Giovannini's vampiress.

A more acceptable film of this type, and one of the few in which the explicit sex scenes are actually a crucial part of the plot, is *Vampyres* (Essay Films), released in 1974. Murray Brown is lured into the clutches of two stunning vampiresses, played by Marianne Morris and Anulka. These two portray to perfection the evil temptress's exploitation of man's weakness for physical attractiveness. Mesmerized, Brown falls in love with one of the vampiresses and is so enslaved by her beauty that he decides to remain with her, despite the downside of this devotion: the nightly depletion of his blood. Inevitably, he is rescued and the thwarted vampiresses perish at daybreak.

Nor was lesbianism excluded from 'swinging' vampire films. The year 1970 saw the release of a film with the self-explanatory title *Vampyros Lesbos* (*Lesbian Vampires*), and also *The Vampire's Lover* (Hammer/AIP), a more tasteful treatment of the subject. Based on Le Fanu's *Carmilla*, itself full of Sapphic connotations, the movie starred the vampire queen of the moment, Ingrid Pitt. As Mircalla Karnstein, she preys upon the innocent Laura (Pippa Steele) with salacious enthusiasm, before getting her just deserts at the hands of Peter Cushing and Douglas Wilmer.

Top left: *The puritanical Peter Cushing destroying a vampire twin in* Twins of Evil, 1971.

Top center: *Peter Cushing holds aloft* Ingrid Pitt's *decapitated head in* The Vampire Lovers, 1970.

Above: *A melodramatic moment in* Twins of Evil, 1971.

Right: L'amante del Vampiro;
beauty is no guarantee of virtue.

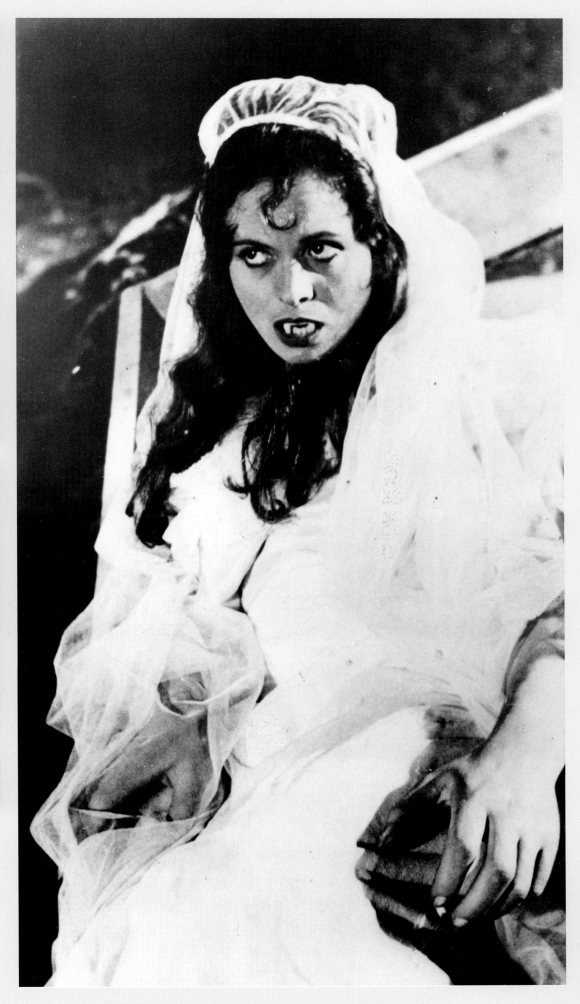

One early female vampire stands out from the rest: Carol Borland, who played daughter to Bela Lugosi's Count Mora in *Mark of the Vampire*, released by MGM in 1935. As the dark-haired, white-clothed, aloof Luna, Borland interpreted the role with serious and detached professionalism. The film was a remake by Tod Browning of his earlier vampire/detective movie *London after Midnight* (1927) and its only weakness is a repetition of the original film's eventual revelation that the vampires are actually flesh-and-blood humans (in this case, actors), masquerading as vampires in order to expose a murderer. Disappointing as this disclosure is, it does not detract from James Wong Howe's wonderful camera work and director Tod Browning's feel for the accoutrements of truly creepy vampire films: swooping bats, scuttling rats and deserted graveyards drenched in moonlight. There is an especially effective scene in which Borland is observed in the castle's chapel gliding silently and gracefully (by means of a concealed harness) through the air, to the accompaniment of organ music. Although later unmasked as an actor, Borland made a most convincing and controlled vampire, in sharp contrast to many of her more specious successors.

It is a sign of its profound success when a genre generates a whole subculture of spoofs. *Dracula* of 1931 was such a phenomenal triumph that it bred firstly a string of similar 'straight' offspring, followed by a multitude of related mutants. It was evident, even in the earlier movies, that Dracula was ripe for spoofing. Lugosi's deadpan portrayal of the Count, and many of his immortal lines ('*I never drink . . . wine*') hinted at the comic possibilities inherent in Dracula movies.

Above: *Elsa Martinelli and Annette Vadim in Roger Vadim's Blood and Roses, 1961; the first lesbian vampire movie.*

Right: *The graceful Carol Borland, 'Countess Luna' in Mark of the Vampire, 1935, which also starred Bela Lugosi.*

Left: *George Hamilton and playmate in the hilarious* Love at First Bite, *1979. Hamilton's Dracula was forced to flee from the family seat in Transylvania when the Communists seized his castle.*

Right: *'Dracula Wants You!' – Bela Lugosi in* Mark of the Vampire.

Below: *Tom Clegg, Fenella Fielding and Kenneth Williams in the dire* Carry on Screaming, *1966.*

Left: *Bela Lugosi was a peerless personifyer of evil, and as such was constantly in demand to play the King Vampire.* Return of the Vampire, 1944.

Above: *Marjorie Weaver and Bela Lugosi, who appeared in vaudeville together.*

As we have seen, Lugosi was to become a victim of his success, being required to reproduce his most famous role time and time again, until his very appearance, whether on-screen or off, became redolent of caricature. Never averse to participating in promotional spin-offs, Lugosi was quite prepared to parody himself in return for remuneration when a suitable occasion arose. Thus, in the 1930s, he played Count Dracula in a vaudeville spoof (which also featured Arthur Treacher and Ed Sullivan), in a 1948 stage show to publicize *Abbott and Costello meet Frankenstein*, and in his own Las Vegas show in 1954, *The Bela Lugosi Review*.

Another screen Dracula, John Carradine, also capitalized on his renown in the role, appearing in a Dracula stage play in the 1950s. At the end of each performance, Carradine took to pronouncing the following question: 'If I'm alive, what am I doing here? On the other hand, if I'm dead, why do I have to wee-wee?' hoping for, and receiving, a cheap laugh.

These semi-official aberrations from the serious business of portraying Dracula as a figure of terror were often condoned by film studios, who were well aware of the thin dividing line between melodrama and spoof, but were also alive to the profits which a comic *Dracula* might realize. Even when a 'serious' *Dracula* film was released, studios often tried to incite the public's interest by using flippant, throwaway lines in their pre-release publicity material. The release of *Dracula Has Risen From the Grave* in 1968, for example, was preceded by this jokey introduction: 'When we last saw him, Dracula was dead with a stake through his heart . . . but you just can't keep a good man down.' Rather than drive spoofs underground, film studios frequently decided to play along with the public enthusiasm for a subversively funny *Dracula*, making spoof movies in the hope of milking this growing cult: there might, after all, be some money to be made from it.

In 1948, Universal-International released *Abbott and Costello meet Frankenstein*, the first in a series of such films, primarily as a vehicle for the talents of Bud Abbott and Lou Costello, the decade's top comedy duo. The film was also an unashamed take-off of *The House of Frankenstein* and *The House of Dracula* (both 1945). Glenn Strange again played Frankenstein's monster, and Lon Chaney Jr. the Wolf Man but, instead of hiring John Carradine, the role of Dracula went to Bela Lugosi – the first time he had appeared as the Count on cinema screens since 1931. While the two funny-men flee in comic confusion from one monster to another, the 'monsters' each play their parts in total solemnity throughout the pandemonium, Lugosi even bettering his performance of 1931. Surprisingly, the comedy/horror formula worked extremely well, the contrasting styles providing a perfect foil for each other.

In 1961, the Mexican film company, Cinematografica Calderon effectively remade the film, appropriating the plot, but substituting Manuel 'Loco' Valdes and Jose Jasso for Abbott and Costello, while Quintin Bulnes played the vampire. Neither *Frankenstein, el Vampiro y Cia* nor Bulnes were worthy challengers, either to the quality of the original film, or to Lugosi.

A dreadful British spoof based on this multiple-monster concept was released in 1966 by Anglo Amalgamated: *Carry On Screaming*. The *Carry On* series, begun in 1958, enjoyed extraordinary popularity and is still repeated on British television to this day, watched with fond amusement by the British public. The same cast was repeatedly employed in dif-ferent scenarios, the proceedings relying heavily on crude lavatorial, sexist and generally basic, humor. Vampirism did not escape this dire, but successful, treatment. Thus, *Carry On Screaming* featured a zombie doctor (Kenneth Williams), Frankenstein's monster (Tom Clegg), a mummy (Dennis Blake) and a female vampire (Fenella Fielding). To the discerning viewer the result has few redeeming features.

By the 1950s, Lugosi had made the switch to comedy and appeared in a British farce whose humor was considered too peculiarly English for release in the United States until the 1960s, when it was retitled *My Son, the Vampire*. *Old Mother Riley Meets the Vampire* (Renown, 1952) was the final film in a series starring the comic transvestite, Arthur Lucan, as an Irish washerwoman and his wife, Kitty McShane, as 'her' daughter. Lugosi played the mad Baron Van Hoosen, who believes himself a vampire and deliberately adopts all the characteristics and paraphernalia of vampirism to bolster his delusion. Sadly, in contrast to *Abbott and Costello meet Frankenstein*, the film is neither particularly funny, nor is Lugosi frightening.

John Carradine was the next erstwhile serious Dracula portrayor to take up the challenge of spoofing the role on film, a challenge it appeared he had been preparing for during his years as a theater Dracula. His opportunity came with the 1965 Circle Productions movie *Billy the Kid vs Dracula*, a spoof version of *Curse of the Undead* (1959). It had been more than two decades since the ageing Carradine had donned the dragon cape on screen, to which he now added a goatee beard and a hefty dose of overacting. This ludicrous combination of west-

Left; *Glenn Strange, Lenore Aubert and Bela Lugosi, united in* Abbott and Costello meet Frankenstein, *1952.*

Right: *Arthur Lucan and Bela Lugosi in* Old Mother Riley Meets the Vampire, *1952.*

Below: *Lou Costello seems unimpressed by Bela Lugosi.* Abbott and Costello meet Frankenstein, *1948. As time went by, Lugosi allowed the vampire image to become part of his real life. He accepted roles in inferior films, sometimes playing a parody of himself.*

Left: *John Carradine and Melinda Plowman in* Billy the Kid vs Dracula, 1965.

Above: *David Niven made an unconvincing vampire in* Vampira, 1974.

Top right: *The unwelcome guest – Christopher Lee in* Tempi Duri per i Vampiri, 1959.

ern and horror film had Dracula preying on the beauteous young Betty (Melinda Plowman), with the uncharacteristically heroic Billy the Kid (Chuck Courtney) surviving shoot-outs and stints in jail before stabbing Dracula with a scalpel. The final result was so awful that, perversely, it has become a cult movie, often screened in conjunction with its equally dreadful successor, *Jesse James Meets Frankenstein's Daughter* (1966).

Lugosi and Carradine had spoofed Dracula years after they had originally become identified with the role, secure in their unassailable reputations as 'serious' Dracula portrayors. Christopher Lee, however, chose to spoof Dracula immediately following his very first film appearance in the role; a somewhat risky venture, even if, as Lee had insisted upon, the vampire he played was not Dracula. Instead, *Tempi Duri per i Vampiri* (*Hard Times for Vampires*), an Italian production released in 1959, featured Lee as Baron Rodrigo, a 'traditional' vampire, who pays an unwelcome and extended visit to his nephew, Count Osvaldo (played by the comic actor, Renato Rascel). The impecunious Osvaldo has been forced to sell his ancestral home and has taken a job as a porter, following its conversion to an hotel. Osvaldo is vampirized by his uncle and rampages through the bedrooms of willing women guests. Unhappily musing 'to bite or not to bite?' Osvaldo finally packs his uncle off, with two nubile girls for company, to the musical strains of *Dracula-cha-cha-cha*. Lee's talents were wasted on this spoof but, thankfully, not to the detriment of his later career as Dracula.

One of the worst examples of Dracula-as-comedy was *Vampira*, released in 1974 by the British film company, World Film Services. Dracula (David Niven) arrives in London, in search of a supply of blood for his beloved wife Vampira (Teresa Graves), and in doing so, takes control of a writer's mind (Nicky Henson). The humor is labored, as are the contrived attempts to bring the action right up to date by introducing busty, 'swinging' wenches, and having the vampiric couple transform into negroes. Niven would have been better advised to stick to his usual portrayals of decent, upright Englishmen.

An altogether worthier offering was *Lady Dracula*, a German production, released in 1977. Barbara (Evelyne Kraft) is the unfortunate vampire who was bitten by Count Dracula when a small girl. Revived in 1976, and commendably reluctant to obtain her 'fix' of blood from human sources, she takes work in hospitals and morgues: anywhere where there is a supply of blood on tap. However, she is eventually driven to prey on humans and in doing so attracts the attention of the police, more particularly an inspector (Brad Harris). The pair are mutually attracted and face some genuinely amusing dilemmas, such as the incompatibility of nocturnal and diurnal lifestyles.

Mama Dracula (a Belgian movie, released in 1979), was loosely based on the Elizabeth Bathory legend. Louise Fletcher plays a countess who regularly bathes in virgins' blood to preserve her fading beauty. Under suspicion from the police, she enlists the services of a Dr Van Bloed (Jimmy Shuman), requesting him to create artificial blood, a respectable, legal alternative to that of virgins. The love interest is provided in the form of a policewoman (Maria Schneider), who ends up marrying both the Countess's twin sons (played by Marc-Henri and Alexander Wajnberg) at once. Never rising above the level of pointless, and unentertaining farce, *Mama Dracula* is a sad disappointment.

By far the best comic vampire film to result from this desire to humorize vampirism must be Simon Productions' *Love at First Bite*, released in 1979. George Hamilton is the handsome, romantically-inclined Dracula, exiled to New York following the appropriation of his Transylvanian castle by the Communists and its subsequent conversion for use as a state gymnasium. In search of love, Dracula is constantly thwarted by the cynicism and neurosis of modern-day America. Finally, his faith in love is restored when he beds an accommodating covergirl (Susan St James). The film is a sophisticated and delightful comedy and as such is untypical of the genre.

Generally, it seemed, neither Dracula, nor his relations, translated that well into comic format. However, one totally off-the-wall CBS-TV situation comedy, now accorded cult status, had great success with its lovable family of monsters. *The Munsters* comprised Herman (a Frankenstein figure), his vampiric wife Lily (Yvonne de Carlo), their werewolf son Eddie (Butch Patrick), their 'normal' all-American niece (Beverly Owen, later played by Pat Priest) and Count Dracula (Al Lewis), Lily's father. The joke was that this oddball collection of freaks regarded themselves as a typical American family, non-threatening and, dare it be said, 'normal'. Al Lewis, a portly figure in Lugosi-like evening dress, complemented by black leather gloves and Jewish accent, had abandoned vampirism for a more absorbing interest in basic scientific experimentation. The whole family presented a cosy, endearing picture, their supernatural characteristics and accoutrements (such as Hermann's coffin-shaped car, affectionately named 'Dragula') being depicted as unremarkable. Although the series was short-lived (1964-66), it is still repeated on television and its popularity generated books, magazines and one film: *Munster Go Home* (Universal, 1966).

Left: *Everyone's favorite Grandpa – Al Lewis in Munster Go Home, 1966.*

Right: *Al Lewis, as Grandpa, Yvonne de Carlo, as Lily, and Fred Gwynne, as Herman: the oddball, eccentric Munsters.*

Below: *The Transylvanian tyrant in one of his more recent incarnations.*

While *The Munsters* was directed at a juvenile audience, *Mad Monster Party?*, released by Embassy Pictures in 1966, aimed at even younger viewers. In this interesting production, all the 'classic' monsters ever screened are brought to life . . . as puppets (designed by Jack Davis). True to form, Count Dracula, now inexplicably sporting a monocle, desperately wishes to eliminate Boris von Frankenstein and thus secure leadership over all the monsters for himself. His dastardly plan is dashed, however, when he, along with the rest of this motley crew, are destroyed by Frankenstein's recently invented explosive. Despite a muddled plot, the film is noteworthy, if only for its novel cast.

In the 60 years since the first screening of *Dracula*, the Count's popularity remains as strong as ever. Since the first realization by film studios of Dracula as a lucrative subject with which to inspire spine-chilling horror among cinema patrons, the Count has continued from strength to strength. Since 1931 he has run the whole gamut of genres and sub-genres: horror, romance, sex and even comedy. While some of these films have had more success than others, his hold on our imagination seems impregnable. His portrayors may change, the situations in which he finds himself may vary from country to continent, from century to century, but this is all part of Dracula's fascination. A true time-traveler, the undead Count's state of immortality enables him to appear whenever and wherever the time and conditions are right for, in Hamilton Deane's words:

When . . . the lights have been turned out and you are afraid to look behind the curtains and you dread to see a face appear at the window – why, just pull yourself together and remember that, after all, *there are such things.*

Transylvanian Trivia

Fangs blinked his blood-red eyes.

'I'm a friendly!' he cried, 'I'm a harmless non-vampire'

But the moment he opened his mouth

His fangs flashed and clashed

FROM *Ffangs the Vampire Bat* BY TED HUGHES

Thanks to the powerful imagination of Bram Stoker and the many and varied efforts of the film industry, the cult of Dracula has become big business. It seems that Dracula has reached out from beyond the grave and has touched nearly every aspect of our lives. Never ones to miss out on a money-spinning opportunity, the marketing men have been there to help him along the way.

Much of the commercial promotion of Dracula has been directed at the juvenile market. Youngsters are encouraged to sink their teeth into Dracula chocolates and ice cream, while the maternal market is sold Dracula cookbooks with which to cater for their offspring. Aside from these culinary delights, nimble-fingered youngsters can exercise their manual dexterity by creating models of Dracula, sold in kits for self-assembly. Halloween is, of course, an ideal occasion on which to dress up in Lugosi-like evening dress and Dracula fangs before embarking upon the important business of trick-or-treating. Young children are familiar with Dracula's presence in their television shows: *The Groovie Goolies*, a cartoon series shown in the early 1970s, was the first to feature 'Cousin Drac' and today even Sesame Street includes a Dracula puppet.

Left: Dracula – the non-threatening version from Sesame Street.

Right: A collection of your favorite monsters – stuffed. Count Bearacula hovers in a cuddly way over Frankenbear and the Bearide of Frankenstein, the Hunchbear of Notre Dame, and the Wolf Bear.

Dracula's persona has been used in numerous television advertisements, endorsing all sorts of incongruous products, while low-quality tabloid newspapers frequently spice up their stories by throwing in a suggestion of vampirism. Much money has been made from Dracula by such media practices, but one cannot help but feel that such trivialization must have Bram Stoker turning in his grave.

More commendably, Dracula's story has been adapted for publication in a variety of forms. Numerous novels and short stories have been written around the character and have been published either as books, or in magazines. Like Dracula films, literary versions of the story appear not only as horror stories, but also as tales of murder, mystery, eroticism and science fiction. The latter category has become particularly popular and continues to flourish. In 1991, for example, Grafton published Brian Aldiss' *Dracula Unbound*, a sci-fi novel which not only features Dracula, but also Bram Stoker, who makes the intriguing revelation that his story is the 'nineteenth century masterwork on syphilis.' A less alarming angle is that taken by Ted Hughes, Britain's Poet Laureate, who has enchanted children with his beautifully illustrated tale of *Ffangs the Vampire Bat* (who is really a small boy who has been bewitched). A notable few of the many modern literary specialists in vampirism include: Anne Rice, Les Daniels, Chelsea Quinn Yarbo, F. Paul Wilson, George R. Martin, Meredith Ann Pierce and Fred Saberhagen, the latter taking a particular interest in updating the *Dracula* story.

The Count has also proved a remarkable success in the world of comics. His first appearance as a comic book monster was in 1953, in *Eerie* magazine, published by Avon Periodicals. *Eerie's* adaptation was virtually a word-by-word reproduction of Stoker's story. However, most comics made use of Dracula as they chose, often relegating him to a secondary role, as in Gold Key Comic's *The Flintstones meet Frankenstein and Dracula*. In 1974, Gold Key's *Daffy Duck* publication even went so far as to include a 'Count Duckula'. As experience with films and novels has shown, it seems that Dracula will never be allowed to remain 'just' Dracula; he is continually being required to appear in increasingly bizarre scenarios in order to further sensationalize his already amazing story.

Nor has Dracula been immune from the attentions of popular music. At first only the accompanying sound-tracks of the best-known Dracula films were released on disc but, during the 1960s and 1970s, the record industry went one step further. Jokey parodies of bona fide pop songs became the rage: *I want to bite your hand* and *Drac the Knife*. The next step was the release of songs especially written about the Count. Bobby 'Boris' Pickett made a career of recording monster songs in the vocal styles of Bela Lugosi and Boris Karloff. His most famous release was *Monster Mash*, but other offerings included *Bela's Bash*, *Transylvanian Twist* and *Blood Bank Blues*.

In a similar vein is the long-running *Rocky Horror Show*, Richard O'Brien's phenomenally successful spoof of teenage horror films. This musical, which had its first showing in the early 1970s, is pure sacrilege for horror pundits. Although the central character, Frank N Furter (immortalized by Tim Curry), is based on Frankenstein, he also incorporates elements of Dracula: '*I'm just a sweet transvestite/From Transsexual/Transylvania/ Why don'tcha stay for the night/ or maybe a bite . . .* ' Irreverent the

92

Left: *A cereal to sink your fangs into: Count Chocula is a choclaty confection of bat and fang shapes.*

Above left: *Vampires are always guaranteed to make the headlines and sell newspapers.*

Left: *Doing the Timewarp at the Annual Transylvanian Convention, The Rocky Horror Picture Show.*

Above right: *David Farrant, self-styled 'High Priest of the Occult Society', conducting a vampire-hunting ceremony in Highgate Cemetery, London. He was jailed in 1974.*

musical may be, but it is also a lively and witty celebration of the worst horror movies. Generations of young people have taken *Rocky Horror* to their hearts and repeatedly attend theater and cinema showings of the production dressed, more often than not, as characters from the musical.

Another Dracula-related development on the pop front was the post-punk and new romantic 'Goth' cult, which took root in Britain in the 1980s. Cult members dressed exclusively in funereal colors, adopting heavy black and white make-up (occasionally relieved by blood-red lipstick), and dying their long hair black. Their preference was for the gloomy, melodramatic rock music which reflected their Gothic image of black romanticism. 'Goth' bands include 'Sisters of Mercy' and 'Bauhaus', the latter group releasing a track entitled *Bela Lugosi's Dead* with the dirge-like refrain, 'Undead, Undead, Undead.'

There are some who take their obsession with the King Vampire even further. Count Dracula societies exist on both sides of the Atlantic, and their organizers publish magazines for an avid readership, award prizes to favored Dracula portrayers and hold theme parties at which their members can consort with fellow fanatics. Their aim is to promote and 'live' the life of their hero, as far as is humanly possible. It may all seem harmless fun, but is often a way of life for members of these societies, stricken with Dracula mania.

For some, however, an obsession with vampirism is not so harmless. Lurid newspaper articles report with depressing regularity on murderous atrocities committed by people convinced that they are vampires. Such killers are frequently diagnosed as schizophrenic, psychotic, psychopathic or afflicted with multiple personality disorder; all psychological conditions which cause the sufferer to really *believe* that he or she is – in many cases – a vampire.

There are a few rational medical theories which have been advanced to explain vampirism. One such hypothesis was put forward by Dr David Dolphin, a Canadian biochemist, in 1985. His belief is that vampirism indeed exists, caused by a variation of porphyria (a condition which, it is believed, 'mad' King George III of England suffered from). According to Dolphin, the disease causes a depletion of the red pigment haem (contained in the haemoglobin of the blood), extreme sensitivity to sunlight, and receding gums, which give the canine teeth the appearance of fangs. Dolphin believes that this haem deficiency causes the sufferer to consume blood in an attempt to compensate.

Another scientist, Dr Stephen Kaplan, believes unequivocably in the existence of vampires, and has even set up a vampire research center in New York to monitor vampirism. As part of his research, he circulates a questionnaire, quizzing known 'vampires' about their lifestyles. Kaplan believes that there are 500 vampires worldwide and has concluded that they are at great risk from AIDS (the flaw in the argument being that since true vampires are already dead, they cannot be affected by any human affliction).

Despite such physiological rationales for vampirism, it is more likely that vampirism *is* merely a myth created by our primitive ancestors in order to explain what they considered otherwise inexplicable occurrences, and perpetuated by the tenacity of superstitious beliefs. To the modern mind, the belief that anyone born on Christmas Day, for example, is a vampire, is totally ludicrous, yet we do not entirely dismiss the notion of vampirism, having been conditioned by our inheritance of centuries of popular folklore.

The most likely explanations for the myth of vampirism are twofold, and rooted in the sad realities of pre-twentieth century life: firstly, the devastating epidemics of the plague, or Black Death, which swept across Europe up until this century. Without the benefit of our advanced medical knowledge, the terrified populace regarded the decimation of their community as the punishment of God, or of the Devil. To the unenlightened mind, the anaemic, weakened state of the victims prior to death could indeed have been put down to vampirism on the rampage (interestingly, in some vampire films, such as *Nosferatu*, the appearance of the vampire coincides with an outbreak of the plague). Indeed, further analogies can be drawn between the vampiric infection and epidemics.

Secondly, there was an appalling frequency of premature burial. Again, without today's medical understanding, the sick were often pronounced dead when, in fact, they were not (a coma, for example, may make the sufferer appear lifeless, although not clinically dead). Such unfortunates were then buried, later to wake up six feet under. Should the graves later be exhumed, for the purpose of seeking out a vampire in his lair, for example, the hunters would find confirmation of their suspicions: bloody injuries caused by the desperate attempt to fight a way out of the suffocating earth, and a corpse which looked much 'fresher' than its presumed date of death should have allowed.

A more positive scientific interest in vampirism was reported in 1991 by the medical journal *Circulation*. The journal published the preliminary findings of an American team of scientists working at the laboratories of Merck, Sharp and Dohme in West Point, Pennsylvania. The team made a detailed study of vampire bats and has succeeded in isolating the gene in the bats' saliva which prevents their preys' blood clotting during a feed. Clearly, this research has important implications for the manufacture of anti-coagulents.

The scholarly side to all this interest in Dracula is not restricted to the medical field alone. Many historians have become fascinated by the genuine historical Dracula, Vlad the 'Impaler'. Radu Florescu and Raymond McNally, academics based in Boston, have made Vlad Tepes their lifes' work. They are the authors of many publications, focusing both on Vlad the 'Impaler' and Stoker's *Dracula*, all of which provide illuminating insights into the awesome historical figure which inspired Stoker's literary character. During the course of their research, they visited modern-day Romania and inspected all the Transylvanian sites associated with Vlad Tepes (including the Chapel of Snagov - Dracula's traditional burial place – and the ruins of the 'real' Dracula's castle on the Arges), and those described so graphically by Stoker.

The Romanian tourist board has recognized Dracula's magnetic attraction to sightseers and offers them 'Dracula tours'. The frequent highlight of these tours is a visit to 'Dracula's castle', Castle Bran which, ironically, was never actually Dracula's castle. The Romanian government, in order to raise hard cash through tourism, has centered its efforts on the regions described by Stoker which, while spectacularly romantic, do not strictly correspond to the haunts of Vlad the 'Impaler'. Thus, while Castle Bran (a thirteenth-century fortress of the Teutonic Order) is indeed the epitome of the archetypal spooky castle, with its turrets and commanding position astride a mountain top, Vlad Dracula's it was not. However, it makes for an infinitely more rewarding visit (and for better snapshots) than the crumbling ruins of the castle on the Arges. Interestingly, the historical Dracula, despite his legendary cruelty and horrendous deeds, is regarded by Romania as a national hero, and officially-erected statues can be found in that country, honoring his memory.

The Dracula myth has become irrevocably incorporated into popular lore and the vampiric Count has become part of our everyday life. Stoker's King Vampire has grown from strength to strength since his creation nearly a hundred years ago, and will undoubtedly continue to do so for, in the Count's own words: 'my revenge is just begun. I spread it over the centuries and time is on my side.'

These pages: *The stuff of which legends are made: a vampire bat, a doll of the medieval ruler Vlad Tepes, the edifice now adopted by the Romanian Tourist Board as Castle Dracula and the masterly Bela Lugosi.*

INDEX

Page numbers in **bold** indicate illustrations.

The publisher would like to thank Adrian Hodgkins the designer, Elizabeth Montgomery the picture researcher, Helen Dawson the indexer, Judith Milidge the editor, and Nicki Giles for production. We are grateful to the following institutions for use of the pictures on the pages noted below:

AA Picture Library: 10-11 top, 10 below.
Thomas G Aylesworth: 14 below, 14-15, 16, 17 below, 23, 30, 42, 61 below, 93 both, 95 below.
The Bettmann Archive: 8, 9 below, 11 below, 17 top, 18, 25 top, 26 top, 27, 28, 37, 43, 46, 48 top, 52, 53, 78, 79, 83, 88, 89 top, 94, 95.
BPL: 2, 4-5, 7, 9 top, 12, 20, 21 top, 22 both, 24 below, 26 below, 29 both, 31 both, 32 both, 33, 34, 35 both, 38 both, 39, 40-41, 44, 45, 47, 48 below, 49, 50, 54, 56, 57 both, 60 both, 61 top, 62, 63, 64, 65 top, 66, 67, 70 both, 71, 72, 74, 75 both, 76 top two, 77, 80 top, 84, 85 below, 86 both, 87, 89 below, 92 below.
British Film Institute: 3, 51, 58-59, 65 below, 68, 69, 73, 80 below, 85 top.
M A C Miles 10 top
Metropolis/Karloffornia: 24 top
Museum of Modern Art/Film Stills Archive: 25 below, 36 top.
National Film Archive, London: 14 (left), 21 below, 36-37, 50 top, 76 below.
National Portrait Gallery, London: 15.
North America Bear Company: 91.
Bill Pierce from Rainbow: 90.
The Theater Arts Harry Ransom Humanities Research Center, University of Texas at Austin: 19 both.
Count Chocula, illustrated on page 92, is a registered trademark of General Mills Inc. and is used with permission.